Smart Guide™
to
Profiting from Mutual Funds

About Smart Guides™

Welcome to Smart Guides. Each Smart Guide is created as a written conversation with a learned friend; a skilled and knowledgeable author guides you through the basics of the subject, selecting out the most important points and skipping over anything that's not essential. Along the way, you'll also find smart inside tips and strategies that distinguish this from other books on the topic.

Within each chapter you'll find a number of recurring features to help you find your way through the information and put it to work for you. Here are the user-friendly elements you'll encounter and what they mean:

⛯ The Keys

Each chapter opens by highlighting in overview style the most important concepts in the pages that follow.

⚡ Smart Money

Here's where you will learn opinions and recommendations from experts and professionals in the field.

💡 Street Smarts

This feature presents smart ways in which people have dealt with related issues and shares their secrets for success.

🏛 Smart Sources

Each of these sidebars points the way to more and authoritative information on the topic, from organizations, corporations, publications, web sites, and more.

📖 Smart Definition

Terminology and key concepts essential to your mastering the subject matter are clearly explained in this feature.

☑ F.Y.I.

Related facts, statistics, and quick points of interest are noted here.

🎓 The Bottom Line

The conclusion to each chapter, here is where the lessons learned in each section are summarized so you can revisit the most essential information of the text.

One of the main objectives of the *Smart Guide to Profiting from Mutual Funds* is not only to better inform you about mutual fund basics, but to make you smarter about investing and finance to ensure a lifetime of security for yourself and your family.

Smart Guide™

to

Profiting from Mutual Funds

Susan Karp

CADER BOOKS

John Wiley & Sons, Inc.

New York • Chichester • Weinheim • Brisbane • Singapore • Toronto

Grateful acknowledgment is made to the following for permission to reprint copyrighted material: Morningstar, Inc. (page 112); State Street Research and Management (pages 129–30); Janus (pages 154–56); T. Rowe Price Associates, Inc. (page 166).

Library of Congress Cataloging-in-Publication Data:
Karp, Susan.
Smart guide to profiting from mutual funds / Susan Karp.
p.   cm.   — (Smart guide)
Includes index.
ISBN 0-471-29609-0
1. Mutual funds—United States. I. Title. II. Series.
HG4930.K36   1998
332.63'27—dc21   98-34845

Printed in the United States of America

10 9 8 7 6 5 4 3 2 1

To my father, for getting me started,
and to Paul, for getting me through

Acknowledgments

This book could not have been written without the help of some remarkably generous individuals: my contributors—Abby Franklin, Christopher Jones, Jim Keener, Mark Mastracci, Charlie O'Bert, Gary Smith, Dick and Eve Vojvoda, and Michele Witten; my "experts"— Susan Belden, Lyle K. Benson, Russ Kinnel, Matt Muehlbauer, Chuck Royce and Jack Fockler of the Royce Funds, Leigh Poggio and Cynthia Liu of Charles Schwab, Jodi Lowe and Brad Tank of Strong Funds, Maria Crawford Scott, John Woerth, and Jack White. Very special thanks go to Martha Conlon of Morningstar Mutual Funds and Bill Dougherty of Kanon Bloch Carré for answering literally dozens of questions. Joy Montgomery, Laura Lorber, Robin Tice, Rowena Itchon, Tisha Findeison, and Jenni Pieratt also provided valuable background information.

My personal thanks to Karen Cashen, John Somerville, Jeanie Ulicny Wilson, and Joel Blum for their contacts and patience; to Elinor Nauen for her advice and common sense; and to Alison Rogers for her "good words."

Contents

Introduction

By the time you read this, there probably will be more than nine thousand mutual funds available to the American investor. So you're not alone if you feel overwhelmed by the sheer volume of possible investment choices.

That's where this book comes in. The goal of the *Smart Guide to Profiting from Mutual Funds* is to help you make sense of the rapidly expanding mutual fund universe. You'll learn how to evaluate both potential investments—and, more important—your own individual financial needs.

The book begins with the basics of mutual fund investing. We all know that funds have grown in popularity; here we find out why. Plus, we'll compare mutual funds with securities and learn just how they stack up to stocks, bonds, and bank investments.

Then we'll take an inside look at the types of funds available. For example, you'll learn the real difference between growth and aggressive growth funds (it's surprisingly less than you might think); the story behind sector funds; the not-so-junky truth about high-yield bond funds; and we'll get to the bottom of the index fund phenomenon.

Most investors are surprised to learn that despite the many funds out there, only a handful are really right for them. That's why this book continually urges you to look at your own life and honestly assess your financial goals, time horizon, and, especially, your personal tolerance for risk.

Throughout the guide, you'll also find profitable advice from investment experts. Newsletter editors, professional money managers, financial planners, and even the lay investor just like yourself share their hard-earned wisdom about making the most of today's markets. They point out what you should look for in a mutual fund and explain smart ways to evaluate fund performance and investment styles. And whether you are looking to invest for retirement, college expenses, a new home, or current income needs, you'll find model asset-allocation plans that can help you to build your own portfolio, one easy step at a time.

Because investing is never a one-time decision, we'll also cover the best ways to manage and monitor your investments. The book includes tips to reading jargon-heavy prospectuses, newspaper fund tables, and often-confusing account statements. We also take a hard look at fund expenses and provide proven strategies to reduce the costs of investing.

There's a good reason the book is titled the *Smart Guide*. It is meant to be used as a resource and designed so that the precise information you need is always easy to find. That's why essential definitions appear right where you need them—not hidden in some back-of-the-book glossary. In addition, "Smart Sources" are included in most chapters, to help you find inexpensive funds, tax help, and places to go for more specific information. And since so many investors have turned to the Internet, you'll also find an up-to-date listing of the best online financial sites.

Investing, particularly in mutual funds, does not have to be either complicated or time consuming. But that does not make it any less important; today more than ever, Americans have to take increasing responsibility for our own financial futures. Fortunately, *you've* already taken the first step to investment success.

CHAPTER 1

·······················

Mutual Fund Basics

THE KEYS

• Professionally managed mutual funds have become America's most popular investment.

• Mutual funds allow you to invest in hundreds of securities for remarkably little money.

• You can invest to meet specific financial goals—whether you want growth, income, or simply to preserve your capital.

• Mutual funds offer one-step diversification—and a host of other advantages.

• Mutual funds can offer better returns than bank CDs with less risk than either stocks or bonds.

America is becoming a nation of investors—and mutual funds are proving to be their investment of choice. Over the past two decades, money has poured into the mutual fund industry to the tune of $4 *trillion*—a sum larger than most countries' economies. And the industry has responded, growing to include more than eight thousand different fund investments.

Chances are, even if you don't own a mutual fund yourself, you know someone who does—a neighbor, co-worker, or relative. In fact, as of 1997, one out of every four American households owned a mutual fund. Or, to put this in a more human context, more Americans have mutual funds than have home computers, car phones, or college educations.

A Brief History

Given their astounding popularity in the United States, it's ironic that mutual funds are actually a nineteenth-century European innovation. Back in the 1870s, Scottish merchants looking for more attractive returns pooled their assets into investment trusts, the forerunner of today's mutual funds. Some of this money eventually found its way to the United States, helping to finance the country's growth after the Civil War.

Of course, nothing succeeds like success, and by the 1920s, the U.S. versions of investment trusts were flourishing. By 1929, investors had a choice of more than seven hundred different investments. Hard hit by the Great Depression (which led to numerous federal reforms that ultimately strengthened the fund business), mutual funds rebounded after World War II—and began to grow into the industry we know today.

Until the early '70s, however, mutual funds remained largely the province of wealthy investors or institutional ones. Middle-income and novice investors relied much more heavily on bank accounts or specific stock investments. But when raging inflation outpaced bank interest rates, Americans went looking for higher-yielding prospects—and fund companies happily provided them. Innovations like money market funds and tax-free funds opened up new opportunities to small investors—and neither they nor the industry has looked back since.

What Is a Mutual Fund?

A mutual fund is an investment company that pools money from many individual investors who share a common or "mutual" investing goal. The fund employs a professional money manager to invest those resources in securities like stocks, bonds, or money market instruments.

Like most corporations, mutual funds issue shares. When you invest in a fund, you own a proportion of the fund's portfolio based on the number of fund shares you own. As a shareholder, you can potentially make money in three ways:

1. You can earn dividends. Dividends are paid from the income that is generated by the fund's investments.

2. You can realize capital gains, when the fund manager sells part of the fund's portfolio for a profit.

3. You can benefit from positive changes in market value. If the value of your fund's portfolio increases or appreciates, so does the value of each share you own. Of course, like most investments, fund share prices can also decrease or depreciate in value as well.

Open and Closed

There are two basic types of mutual funds: *open-end funds* and *closed-end funds*. Open-end funds are by far the more common; they're what most of us mean when we talk about mutual fund investments. Open-end funds continually issue (and buy back) shares to meet investor demand. The share price of an open-end fund is determined by the market value of the securities held by the fund's portfolio.

Closed-end funds, on the other hand, issue a fixed number of shares, which generally trade on an exchange, much like a corporate stock. That's why the price of closed-end funds depends not just on the fluctuating value of the fund's portfo-lio, but also on the market demand for fund shares.

While there are some good reasons to invest in closed-end funds (for example, they're often traded at a discounted price), they're much more complicated to buy, sell, and research than open-end investments, and aren't necessarily suitable for most investors. This book will focus solely on

Fidelity:
The First Name in Stock Funds

Boston-based Fidelity may well be America's best-known mutual fund company; it's certainly the largest. Fueled by the stunning success of its Magellan Fund, Fidelity now has more than $600 billion under management and offers more than two hundred mutual funds.

Founded in 1946 by stockpicker Ned Johnson, Fidelity has always emphasized extensive research and a "bottom-up" investing approach that concentrates on specific companies rather than overall industries. This strategy paid off with tremendous returns throughout the 1980s and early 1990s; however, the family has stumbled in recent years. Critics charge that Fidelity's mammoth size has made it difficult for the company to implement the bold moves it was once famous for. Highly publicized fund manager defections have also hurt. However, a recent flurry of proactive management moves—like closing the now $60-billion-plus Magellan to new investors—have won kudos from the industry.

Investors interested in Fidelity funds may want to check out one of the many independent newsletters that analyze the company's offerings. Fidelity Insight, created by ex-staffer Eric Kobren, is available by calling (617) 369-2500; the equally comprehensive Fidelity Monitor is at (800) 397-3094.

Fidelity Investments
800-544-8888
www.fidelity.com

open-end funds; however, more information about closed-end funds is available from the Investment Company Institute, a Washington, D.C.-based industry association. The ICI can be reached at (202) 326-5800 or via their web site (www.ici.org).

Prospectus

A prospectus is a legal document that contains important information about the fund's objectives, investment strategy, and fees. The Securities and Exchange Commission (SEC) has mandated that fund companies must provide a prospectus to all potential fund investors.

Choose Your Goal: Investing for Growth, Income, or Safety

Every mutual fund, whether open- or closed-end, invests to meet a specific financial objective, which is described in the fund's prospectus. You'll find that a fund's goals are usually very broad; most fall into one of three categories:

• **Growth.** The fund manager seeks to increase the value of fund assets

• **Income.** The manager aims to generate a regular flow of current income

• **Safety.** The manager aims simply to protect your money from loss

A fund's objective should provide you with a general guide to how the fund will invest (although you'll be surprised to learn how loosely some fund managers can interpret these simple definitions). Funds seeking growth will invest mainly in stocks, which have historically outperformed all other investments, delivering the best returns over time. Stock funds come in many varieties: aggressive growth funds; growth-and-income funds; small-company funds; international funds; specialized or sector funds; index funds; and many (some might say too many) more. You'll find more information about stock funds in chapter 2.

Income funds, not surprisingly, focus primarily on bonds and other dividend-paying securities (including stocks) in order to generate a steady income stream. Quite a number of bond funds also offer tax advantages: by investing in instruments issued by the United States or by municipal governments, they can provide returns exempt from local, state, and even federal taxes.

Investors looking for stability tend to prefer money market funds, also known as money funds. These funds typically invest in high-quality, short-term securities, such as U.S. Treasury Bills and bank certificates of deposit; many provide tax-free income as well. Managed to maintain a constant $1 share price, money funds provide a remarkably high degree of safety (although it's important to note that they are neither guaranteed nor insured by the federal government). We'll discuss both bond and money funds in more depth in chapter 3.

SMART DEFINITION

Stocks
Stocks represent an ownership stake in a corporation. By purchasing shares of stock, you buy a fraction of that company; consequently, you stand to profit if and when the company makes money.

The Advantages of Fund Investing

For some, the attractive returns delivered by so many mutual funds over the past few years are justification enough to invest. But mutual funds also offer a host of special advantages, particularly for the individual investor:

• **Professional money management.** Have you ever wanted to hire a full-time financial adviser to look after your assets? That's essentially what you're doing when you invest in a mutual fund—only for a lot less money.

For a surprisingly small sum (usually for as little as a $1,000 investment), an experienced fund

SMART DEFINITION

Bonds

Bonds are basically IOUs issued by government agencies or corporations. When you buy a bond, you're essentially lending money. In exchange for the loan, you earn interest over a fixed period of time, which can range from a few months to thirty years or even longer.

manager effectively evaluates the markets for you, seeks out the best opportunities in which to invest your money, monitors your portfolio regularly, and determines exactly when to buy and sell your stocks or bonds.

Because they're usually backed by an extensive research staff, portfolio managers often know about attractive companies or market sectors long before laypeople do. Many managers are experts in specialized fields, such as technology or foreign markets. Some are simply phenomenal stock pickers, like the legendary Peter Lynch, formerly of Fidelity's Magellan Fund.

Personality certainly isn't everything when it comes to choosing a mutual fund. But whether your fund is run by a star manager or an unheralded team of advisers, they undoubtedly all have access to more information and trading resources than just about any individual investor.

• **Built-in diversification.** "Diversification" simply means spreading your money among different investments. Over the years, studies have shown that by not putting all your eggs in one basket—or all your dollars in one asset—you can significantly reduce your investment risk, offsetting losses from one security with gains in another.

Most mutual funds provide you with one-step diversification. The average stock fund, for example, invests in a hundred or so different securities; the average bond fund in more than seventy different issues. So a decline in any single holding should have a minor impact on the fund's portfolio as a whole. Many mutual funds take diversification even further, investing across industry classes, market sectors, or even different countries. It is not difficult to imagine how very expensive (and time-consuming) that would be to achieve on your own.

Two types of nondiversified—or at least less diversified—mutual funds have recently become popular: *sector funds* and *concentrated funds.* Sector funds specialize in a single market segment, like financial services or real estate. Concentrated funds typically don't have a specific market focus, but like sector funds, will invest in an extremely limited number of companies. While these funds can achieve sometimes spectacular returns, they're much less able to weather market or industry fluctuations than funds with a wider investment base.

• **Ready access to your money.** If you already own stocks or bonds or even your own home, you know how difficult it can be to turn that asset into fast cash. Buyers need to be found and sales transacted.

But mutual funds are remarkably liquid investments. You can easily buy or sell shares on any

F.Y.I.

On-site visits help many fund managers assess a company's products or future performance. The Robertson Stephens Global Resources Fund actually has a staff geologist to help evaluate investment opportunities.

Which Fund Is Right for You?

Your Goal	Suggested Investments
Saving for Retirement	Aggressive Growth Funds (page 25)
Buying a House	Growth Funds (page 27)
Day-to-Day Income	Bond or Equity Income Funds (pages 57, 30)
Paying Fewer Taxes	Tax-Free Municipal Bond Funds (page 65)
"Parking" Money You'll Need in a Few Months' Time	Money Market Funds (page 69)

F.Y.I.

Watch out for mutual funds that are really sector funds in disguise. For example, the White Oak Growth Fund invests an astounding 66 percent of its portfolio in technology stocks—more than most self-proclaimed tech funds. Stellar performance has attracted investors, but a downturn in the computer industry could wreak havoc with fund returns.

business day, usually with a phone call. In fact, unlike a company whose stock you own, the mutual fund itself will buy your shares back from you. Of course, like the value of most securities, the value of fund shares will fluctuate daily. When redeemed, your investment may be worth less or more than its original purchase price.

• **Low minimum investment.** They're probably the most cost-effective of all investments; with very little money, you can own hundreds of securities. Just try doing that with individual stocks.

Today, you can buy into even the best-performing funds for as little as $1,000 (even less if you're investing in a retirement account such as an IRA). And you can add to your holdings in even smaller increments.

No wonder mutual funds are often highly recommended to beginning investors—although they're just as attractive for people with greater resources at their disposal.

• **Wide range of investment choices.** While the number of funds now available may seem overwhelming at first, having so many choices can actually make it easier to find investments that suit your exact needs.

Mutual funds can invest to achieve very broad objectives, such as long-term growth or short-term security. But they can also have a very specific focus—for example, tax-free income, a particular market segment, or even a foreign country.

In fact, mutual funds can provide remarkably easy entrée to some of today's more volatile (but often high-performing) markets. For example, while international investments can be a terrific way to diversify your portfolio, most individuals don't

Invest for Less:
Funds with Minimal Minimums

You don't need a lot of money to start investing in the mutual fund world. The following top-rated funds can be purchased for anywhere from $50 to $500.

Fund Name	Minimum Initial Purchase
Alliance Growth & Income 800-227-4618	$250
American Mutual 800-421-4120	$250
Excelsior Value & Restructuring 800-446-1012	$500
Fidelity Destiny 800-752-2347	$50
Homestead Value 800-258-3030	$500
Investment Company of America 800-421-4120	$250
MAP-Equity 800-559-5535	$250
Munder Index 500 800-438-5789	$500
Nicholas 800-227-5987	$500
Wachovia 800-994-4414	$250

Source: Morningstar, Inc.

What Is a Hedge Fund?

Once solely the province of the ultra, ultra rich, hedge funds have lately been gaining popularity among many higher-income investors as well. Valued as much for its financial cachet as its potential for spectacular returns, today's hedge fund is more like an exclusive private investment club than the ordinary—more democratic—mutual fund.

Largely unregulated, these very limited investment partnerships can employ extremely speculative strategies, such as shorting stocks, leveraging assets and betting on foreign currency movements. In fact, because of the much greater risks involved, the Securities and Exchange Commission (SEC) has required that hedge fund investors be "accredited," which simply means that you need either a net worth of at least $1 million or an annual income of $200,000 or more ($300,000 for married couples). Not surprisingly, the opening ante for a hedge fund is substantially higher than that of most securities; the usual minimum investment can range anywhere from $250,000 to $500,000.

But before you dash off a check, make sure you understand just what you're getting into. Certainly some hedge funds (particularly those run by legendary financier George Soros) have delivered mind-blowing average annual returns of as much as sixty or seventy percent. Others, however, have fallen prey to their own high-flying strategies. Just last year, hedge fund manager Victor Niederhoffer actually lost all of his investors' money, thanks to bad gambles on the Thai baht and stock-index futures.

Obviously, if you're interested in (or eligible for) a hedge fund, you should seek out more information than this book can provide. Two internet resources, the Hedge Funds Home Page (www.hedgefunds.net) and Anakonda (www.anakonda.com) offer general definitions as well as links to fund providers.

have the time or expertise to evaluate solid overseas companies. However, by tapping the resources of an international or global fund manager, even the most inexperienced investor can take advantage of these decidedly more complicated opportunities.

How Do Mutual Funds Compare with Other Investments?

Given their advantages, it's not surprising that mutual funds have become one of today's most popular investment vehicles, for both institutional investors (who enjoy substantial financial clout) and individuals.

But it's important to understand that mutual funds aren't the Holy Grail of investing. They're not foolproof—nor are they marketproof. In fact, during an overall market decline, even the most diversified mutual funds are likely to drop in value. Remember, a mutual fund is simply made up of many stocks and bonds; if the individual securities fluctuate, so will your fund's portfolio. The expectation is that the bounce will be lessened because the fund has so many different holdings.

Of course, not every investment is right for every investor. Before you invest in any security, mutual funds included, do a little comparison shopping. Knowing what other possibilities are available can help you make better choices when it comes to investing your own money.

Bank Certificates of Deposit

The best thing that can be said about bank accounts is that they're boring—which is actually quite a compliment. Backed by federal insurance, bank CDs are guaranteed (not a word usually associated with investing) to protect your assets. You can sleep

F.Y.I.

Are you worrying about the "wrong" risk? In the long run, investing too conservatively could hurt you even more than a stock market plunge. If your returns aren't keeping pace with inflation, you'll never meet your investing goals.

SMART DEFINITION

Credit Quality
Credit quality is a measure of the financial strength of the bond issuer and its ability to repay its debts. To help investors evaluate a bond's creditworthiness, bonds are rated from AAA or Aaa (highest quality) to D (in default). Standard & Poor's Corporation and Moody's Investors Service are the two best-known bond-rating agencies.

more easily with this type of investment, knowing that you won't lose a penny.

Of course, you won't earn that much, either. Unfortunately, safety doesn't pay very well; over time, a CD's rate of return is likely to be lower than the *potential* return on almost every other type of investment.

And unlike mutual funds, CDs aren't very liquid investments. Generally, you can't cash in your CD before its maturity date without having to pay penalties. However, if you like the stability of CDs but would rather not tie up your cash for long periods, you may be interested in investing in money market funds. Money markets are a type of mutual fund that holds shorter-term, high-quality securities, including certificates of deposit and Treasury Bills. They provide the same guarantee of principal, but can be redeemed at any time. You'll find more information about money market funds in chapter 3.

Treasury Securities

Talk about a secure investment: Treasuries are backed by the full faith and credit of the U.S. government and therefore are considered virtually free from any risk of default. They also provide regular income exempt from both state and federal taxes.

There are three kinds of Treasuries. Short-term Bills are available in maturities ranging from three months to one year and have a hefty $10,000 minimum requirement. Intermediate-term Notes mature in two to ten years (shorter-term Notes sell for $5,000, and longer-term Notes—those maturing in more than five years—sell for $1,000). And long-term Bonds, which also sell for $1,000, mature in eleven to thirty years' time.

While numerous mutual funds invest in Treasury securities, it's often better to own these investments outright; that way, you avoid having to pay fund expenses that can erode income. Remember, the government's assurance means you don't need the protection of a widely diversified portfolio: you're guaranteed to get back at least 100% of your original investment. However, because Treasuries are affected by the same interest rate risks that affect any bond, many financial advisers recommend mixing maturities, and buying a handful of issues that come due at different times.

Individual Bonds

Issued by governments, banks, or corporations, these debt obligations offer a steady stream of guaranteed or "fixed" interest payments (bonds are often referred to as fixed income investments).

Credit quality is key to bond returns. The more likely an issuer is to default, the higher the interest rate the bond will pay (which is why "junk" bonds are also known as high-yield bonds). Because bond funds can invest in a wide variety of bond issues—ranging from extremely safe Treasuries to the most speculative of corporate bonds—investors are often better protected from the risk of default than they would be with an individual security. And with much lower investing minimums—bond fund investments can be as low as $500, rather than the $5,000 investment required for a typical bond—bond funds offer a more affordable way to take advantage of bond market movements.

Speaking of market movements: Although bonds are traditionally considered more conservative investments than stocks, they're far from risk-free. Bond prices will drop when interest rates rise (and vice versa); in 1994, six separate interest rate hikes played havoc with bond returns (*including* those of Treasury securities). That year, bond and bond fund investors found themselves holding securities that had suddenly dropped substantially in value.

Individual Stocks

Diversification can be a double-edged sword; while investing in many stocks reduces the damage that can be inflicted by any one declining security, it also dilutes the positive impact any spectacularly performing company can have on the portfolio's overall return.

Stocks are considered wealth builders for good reason: they can grow more dramatically than just about any other investment. Early investors in the computer company Netscape watched the stock rise from $58 to $100 to $160 within the first six months of trading—an increase of 175 percent.

Obviously, discovering the next Netscape isn't easy, or we'd all be millionaires or mutual fund managers. Not surprisingly, there are many more losers on the stock market than there are obvious winners (in fact, Netscape itself has suffered substantial reversals since its first high-flying days). And stock trading does come at a price; even a relatively inexpensive $20 stock would end up costing you $2,000 for the traditional "round lot" (100 shares) plus a 10 percent to 30 percent brokerage commission.

Individual stocks certainly have a place in your portfolio, particularly if you're knowledgeable about a specific company or industry. But be prepared to invest significant amounts of both time and money. Unlike a stock fund investor, who can rely on a professional money manager, you'll really be on your own when it comes to researching and monitoring individual securities.

THE BOTTOM LINE

No wonder mutual funds have become so popular: they offer small investors access to the financial advantages once limited to wealthy or institutional investors. Mutual funds pool the resources of many people to invest in a diversified portfolio of securities, which is then managed by a financial professional.

Whether you choose stock, bond, or money market funds, you'll enjoy reduced investment risk, potentially attractive returns, and ready access to your money. Mutual funds also compare well to other investments, offering greater returns than CDs with less risk than either individual stocks or bonds.

CHAPTER 2

········

Stock Funds

• Stocks have outperformed all other investments for more than seventy years. No wonder experts recommend that stocks or stock funds should be a part of every investor's portfolio.

• Stocks may offer greater growth potential, but that does come with greater risks.

• A wide spectrum of choices—from aggressive growth to sector investing—makes it easy to find funds that fit your specific needs.

To investors, the 1990s have proven to be the decade of the bull—the bull market, that is. Thanks to the spectacular performance of both the domestic and international stock markets, even the most casual investor is now well aware of the dramatic growth potential of stocks—and, consequently, of stock funds.

Since 1991, the U.S. stock market has delivered average annual returns of more than 16 percent; in 1997 alone, the market gained an astounding 33 percent. Although veteran market watchers have cautioned that these numbers are unusually—even abnormally—high, history is still

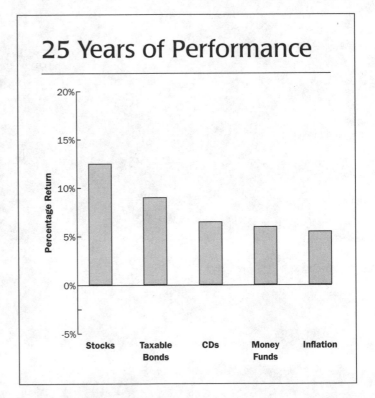

25 Years of Performance

Sources: Bank Rate Monitor, the Federal Reserve, *Money Fund Report,* Lehman Bros., Standard & Poor's

on the side of the stock investor. Since 1926, stocks have outperformed all other investments, outpacing CDs, bonds, government securities, and, most important, the rate of inflation, by a dramatically wide margin. No wonder stocks are considered wealth builders, the only investment vehicles with the power to keep you both ahead of inflation and on target to meet even the most ambitious financial goals.

Of course, as fund companies are obliged to warn, past performance is no guarantee of future returns. But while stocks are unlikely to continue growing at their current torrid pace, they're almost certain to come out ahead over the long term.

Why? By investing in a stock, you're not only investing in a security; you're making an investment in a company, betting on its chances for growth and future success. And that success can be meteoric. Just think of Microsoft or Dell Computer, two relatively young companies that have now become household names and investing blockbusters.

While stocks offer nearly limitless growth potential, bonds, by contrast, simply pay down an IOU. So at best, bond investors can expect only repayment of their principal investment plus a guaranteed rate of interest. While this return may be attractive and is certainly predictable, there's no real opportunity for your money to grow any further.

SMART DEFINITION

Bull Market
Markets move in cycles, sometimes up and sometimes down. "Bull market" simply means an upward trend in the price of stocks or other securities. Bull markets can last for years; however, sooner or later, the bulls will be followed by the bears. Bear markets are periods when overall prices decline and the market as a whole trends downward.

SMART MONEY

The stock market's recent performance has been unusually robust. Chuck Royce, chief investment officer at the Royce Funds, recommends that investors temper their expectations for the future. "Instead of the twenty percent to thirty percent returns of the past few years, investors should expect more normal returns in the range of minus five percent to plus fifteen percent.

While this may sound discouraging in the short term, it could lead to enormous investment opportunities in the future. A higher level of market volatility often results in the irrational pricing of securities, which causes undervalued or bargain opportunities to emerge."

The Risk/Reward Trade-Off

Before you count your stock market profits, remember that market averages are exactly that—an average that includes (some might say masks) tremendous fluctuations in performance. The same investors who enjoyed the stock market's amazing 37.5 percent gain in 1995 probably suffered through the previous year's dismal 1.3 percent return as well. And who can forget 1997's historic one-day Dow Jones Industrial Average plunge of more than 550 points?

In the market, what goes up can just as frequently come down. That's the risk you take in order to achieve inflation-beating returns. Risk and reward are really two sides of the same coin; in general, the more risk you take on, the greater your potential reward—as well as the larger your potential loss.

Risk should not be underestimated; no matter how strong a stomach you may have, it's still frightening to watch your portfolio plunge 20 percent or more in a single day. (Think that's far-fetched? Investors who were around for 1987's "Black Monday" saw a $10,000 investment shrink to just over $7,700, on average, by the end of that trading day.) However, as we'll see in chapter 4, there are relatively easy ways for even fainthearted investors to strike a comfortable balance between risk and reward.

Risks to Watch Out For

It's important to remember that *every* investment decision you make involves some form of risk, whether you choose the most aggressive mutual fund or a savings account at your neighborhood bank. While a federally insured and guaranteed CD may preserve every penny of your principal, it can't protect you from inflation risk, which is the very real possibility that inflation will rise faster than your investment earnings, leaving you with less purchasing power than you had when you started.

But most investors are more concerned with what is called market risk—the possibility that the stock market will suffer a decline and their investment will consequently lose money. It's certainly not unheard-of for an individual stock to lose 50 percent or even 100 percent of its value, although thanks to diversification, that can rarely, if ever, happen to a mutual fund. But it's important to remember that the uncertainty and volatility of the stock market are exactly what produce the opportunity for investment growth—and the possibility of higher returns.

Making Sense of the Stock Fund Universe

Given their tremendous potential for growth, it's not surprising that there is a huge number of stock funds available. As a matter of fact, with nearly five thousand funds to choose from, the number of stock funds now exceeds the number of securities

What should you look for in a stock fund? Susan Belden, editor of the *No-Load Fund Analyst* newsletter, advises: "First, think beyond short-term performance. We've found that one good year doesn't prove much about a fund; it could just be luck. We like to focus on longer-term records, and advise people to take at least a five-year view.

"In fact, numbers are just our first screen. We're more interested in following fund managers than funds per se. We look for managers who offer a well-thought-out and disciplined approach. Consistency both of returns and investing style is really key."

listed on the New York and American Stock Exchanges *combined.*

Taken as a whole, the stock fund universe can seem overwhelming. But this much choice means you can find funds that not only meet your specific investing needs but also match your personal comfort with risk.

Today, stock funds span the risk spectrum, from the relatively conservative to the downright speculative. While new funds—and fund categories—seem to be popping up every day, we will discuss seven basic varieties:

- Aggressive growth funds

- Growth funds

- Equity income funds

- Total-return funds

- Index funds

- Specialty or sector funds

- International funds

These seven broad categories reflect the typical investing objectives of most mutual funds and are certainly a good place to begin; however, investors will soon discover the unfortunate truth that the fund industry itself doesn't use any standard classification. In fact, what category a fund is assigned to will likely vary depending on what ratings service, newspaper, or investing site is doing the categorization.

Aggressive Growth Funds

No category illustrates the risk/reward trade-off as well as aggressive growth funds. Seeking maximum returns, these aptly named funds also take maximum chances, investing in very rapidly growing companies in order to achieve their often staggering returns. In 1991, this category of mutual fund gained more than 50 percent; on

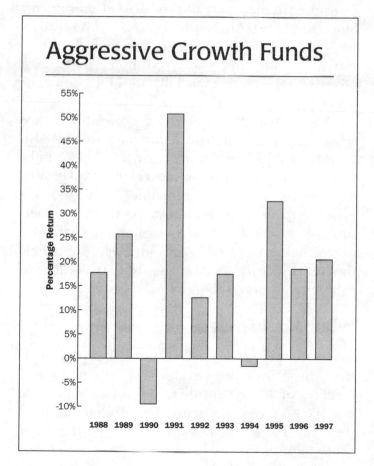

Source: Kanon Bloch Carré

the other hand, performance fell by more than 25 percent in 1987.

Undervalued stocks are favorites of aggressive growth fund managers; they look for promising if unproven new companies, or industries that have fallen out of favor. They can also engage in somewhat risky strategies, like selling short or buying on margin. Aggressive growth funds rarely make income or dividend distributions; their returns come entirely from increases in the share prices of the companies they hold.

Leaders during booming markets, these funds can suffer dramatically during market downturns. Since the best returns usually come to funds that stay fully invested in stocks at all times rather than retreating to safer cash positions, aggressive growth funds can be especially hard hit when markets tumble.

A subcategory of aggressive growth funds are those that invest in small-company stocks. Also known as small-capitalization or small-cap funds, these investments aim for extremely fast growth by investing in young companies with attractive growth prospects. Small-cap stocks frequently perform well when their larger-cap counterparts are out of favor, and vice versa; however, given their tiny size and lower trading volumes, small-caps are substantially more volatile.

Who Should Invest

Investors with strong nerves and financial goals that are at least five years away. With occasional declines of 20 percent or more not only possible but likely, these funds are best suited to those investing for far-off college tuition payments or retirement accounts.

Who Shouldn't Invest

Fainthearted investors or those who want regular income payments would do well to stay far, far away. Small-caps are also not recommended for investors with shorter-term needs, who might have to tap into the money in a year or two.

Growth Funds

With similar objectives—albeit moderately different tactics—growth funds are the more cautious cousin of aggressive growth investments. Although they also favor fast-growing companies, these funds generally tend to concentrate on larger and better-established stocks. Because of this, growth funds will usually achieve attractive if not eye-popping returns (although growth funds actually outperformed their more aggressive counterparts in 1997). More important, though, these funds are much better able to weather market fluctuations; while they'll still dip during down markets, they usually don't fall quite as far as aggressive growth funds.

Since capital appreciation is their main goal, growth funds offer little dividend income. However, because they offer tremendous growth potential with a reasonable amount of risk, growth funds are key to any investor's success, and have a place in even the most conservative portfolios.

It's important to be careful, though, when choosing a growth fund. Many so-called growth funds take just as many risks as and in fact invest in the same stocks as, more aggressive funds. Make sure that you not only read the fund's prospectus

F.Y.I.

Are small-cap stocks too big for you? Micro-caps are one of today's fastest-growing fund categories. The average micro-cap company has a market capitalization of $200 million. Compare that to computer giant IBM, whose market cap is more than $50 *billion*.

but also get a sense of the fund's portfolio before you commit any money. Key things to look for are a preponderance of familiar names (Wal-Mart, Merck, and Microsoft are typical holdings) that span a wide range of industries.

Focusing on Focused Funds

We briefly mentioned focused (or concentrated) funds in chapter 1. These relative newcomers have become increasingly popular in the last year or so; in fact, many well-known fund companies, including trend-wary Vanguard, now offer some variation on the theme.

What focused funds are focusing on are the best ideas of fund managers. Unlike most mutual funds, these portfolios are small (some would even say tiny), typically holding fewer than forty different securities. And therein, of course, lies the potential downside. While a few good stock picks can result in tremendous returns, a few bad ones can just as easily spell disaster. Even one of the best-regarded focus funds, the Janus Twenty Fund, suffered through a prolonged ugly spell during the early 1990s, despite achieving annualized ten year gains of more than 20 percent.

That's not to say these funds don't have a place in your portfolio. Achieving double-digit performance is always appealing (just ask investors who benefited from the Oakmark Select Fund's sizzling 55 percent return in 1997). But don't let one-year performance figures blind you to the substantial risks of undiversified funds. Even their managers would recommend balancing a focused fund investment with less aggressive choices.

Focused Fund Choices

Janus Twenty (800-525-3713)
Oakmark Select (800-625-6275)
Safeco Growth (800-426-6730)
Vanguard Selected Value (800-662-7447)
White Oak Growth Stock (800-932-7781)

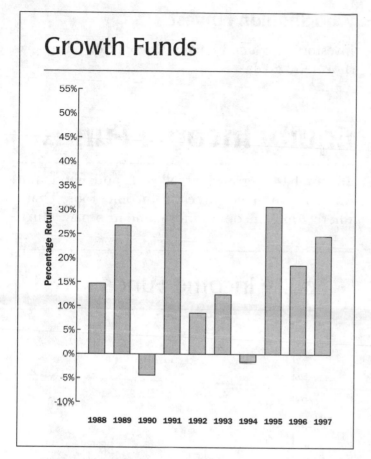

Growth Funds

Source: Kanon Bloch Carré

Who Should Invest

Investors willing to take a long-term perspective and stay put even through the inevitable down markets. However, a good growth fund should be a core holding for anyone with more than a one- to two-year time frame. Look for funds that invest mostly in large- or mid-cap stocks.

Who Shouldn't Invest

Investors who need current income or have very short-term goals.

Equity Income Funds

To emphasize growth is all well and good, but what if you need to earn income too? That's where equity income funds come into play. Much

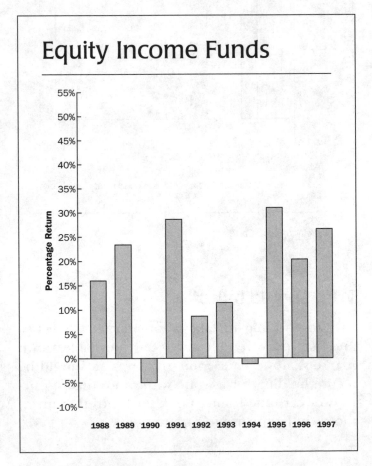

Equity Income Funds

Source: Kanon Bloch Carré

more conservative than either variety of growth fund, equity income funds concentrate on providing regular income payments while offering the chance of solid if not substantial gains.

Equity income funds invest heavily in stocks that offer relatively high, predictable dividend payments. These companies tend to be large and established, without the wild swings you typically find with more aggressive growth stocks. That makes equity income funds a more stable bet in uncertain or declining markets. Ideal for older investors, these funds offer attractive income without sacrificing growth potential, and are an appealing alternative to a straight bond fund.

Who Should Invest

Investors looking for predictable income without giving up growth will find these an ideal addition to their portfolio. Risk-averse investors will also find that these funds are less sensitive to dramatic market fluctuations.

Who Shouldn't Invest

Emphasizing income over performance, these funds are probably a bit too conservative for investors with aggressive long-term goals, although they can add needed stability to an otherwise volatile portfolio.

Total-Return Funds

This umbrella term refers to at least three comparable types of mutual funds: growth-and-income funds, balanced funds, and asset allocation funds.

F.Y.I.

Investors who want to emulate Wall Street legend Warren Buffett—or at least take advantage of his value-oriented philosophy—may be interested in the Focus Trust Fund. Managed by Buffett's biographer Robert Hagstrom, the fund invests in many Buffett-endorsed stocks. But these picks seem to have been more successful for the master than for his disciple: as of 1997, Focus Trust trailed both the Standard & Poor's 500 market index and its fund category.

All have the same objective—a balance of income payments and steady growth—but each gets there in a slightly different way.

Of the three, *growth-and-income funds* invest most heavily in stocks, primarily those of well-established companies that can offer either growth potential or reliable dividend income. Similar to equity income investments (although less risky), growth-and-income funds offer the lowest income yields of the total-return group with overall better performance.

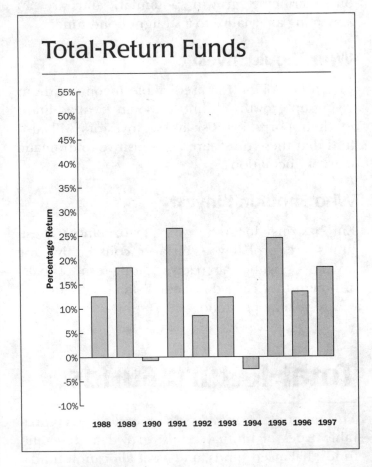

Total-Return Funds

Source: Kanon Bloch Carré

American Funds: The Quiet Giant

American who? You're not alone if you don't recognize the name of the third-largest mutual fund company in the country. Although this Los Angeles–based investment manager can boast of more than $200 billion in shareholder assets, it rarely does. But ducking the spotlight hasn't hindered either its performance or its popularity. Even though they're sold primarily through brokers and financial planners, American's best-known stock funds—Investment Company of America ($39.7 billion in assets), Washington Mutual Investors ($45.8 billion in assets), and EuroPacific Growth ($21.3 billion in assets)—rank among the fifteen biggest and have provided consistently outstanding long-term returns.

American believes in a team approach to fund management, which assures continuity of both style and objective. Minimizing risk is another company trademark. But while American does offer some of the best-regarded funds in the industry, investors should be aware that they are also some of the most expensive, charging hefty fees of more than 6 percent of your investment.

American Funds
800-421-0180
www.americanfunds.com

Balanced funds operate almost as two separate portfolios, one investing in stocks and the other in interest-paying securities like bonds. Typically, balanced funds (also known as hybrid funds) keep anywhere from 50 percent to 70 percent of their portfolio in equities and 30 percent to 50 percent in bonds. Offering the most income of all stock funds, balanced funds also provide a tremendous amount of stability in declining markets. Their fixed-income component, which can result in lower returns during booming markets, helps cushion the effects of market declines.

Asset allocation funds have gained tremendous popularity in recent years. These funds offer a diversified portfolio through a single fund investment; they split their holdings among stocks, bonds, and cash, although each fund manager obviously has leeway over the exact percentages. Not surprisingly, these funds are never the market's top performers; however, they do hold up quite well during volatile periods.

Who Should Invest

Investors who are concerned about risk or don't want to think about creating a diversified portfolio on their own. Despite trading off high growth potential for income, these funds have actually performed well during the recent bull market, and should continue to hold their value during the next bearish cycle.

Who Shouldn't Invest

Investors whose portfolios are already well diversified have no need for a total-return fund. The middle-of-the-road approach will only frustrate those seeking bigger gains.

Index Funds

Equity index funds have hogged the headlines lately. Thanks to a booming stock market, these funds—which simply invest in the securities that make up a particular market index, such as the S&P 500—have been outperforming nearly every active portfolio manager on Wall Street. In 1997, in fact, index funds outpaced 90 percent of all stock funds; the year before, they outperformed 74 percent of the entire stock fund universe.

With this kind of track record, why bother with actively managed funds at all? Because the market doesn't always boom; investors with longer memories well recall the pain of sharp market downturns. And not surprisingly, index funds, which simply track market behavior, head south when the market does. Go back only as far as 1993, when 68 percent of portfolio managers beat the market, or 1992, when 59 percent did,

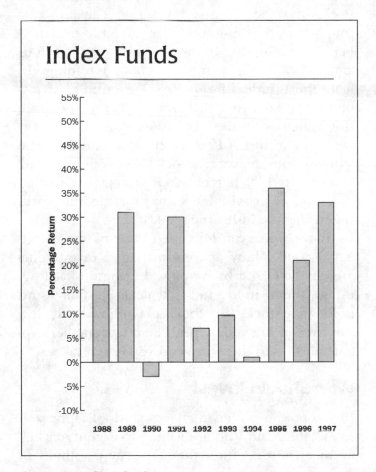

Index Funds

Source: Kanon Bloch Carré

to appreciate the value added by a good fund manager.

That said, index funds can be a terrific opportunity, particularly for beginning investors. In fact, they're often recommended to fulfill the large-company-stock component of a well-diversified portfolio. (Index funds that track small companies have actually been proven less effective; active fund managers seem to be better able to unearth promising young stocks than an index can.)

Costs, or the lack thereof, are a big reason for the success of index funds. Because they're passively managed—that is, they choose investments simply by matching the mix of an established benchmark—index funds can save a tremendous amount of money on research and trading. In fact, most index funds have astoundingly low operating expenses; the granddaddy of them all, the Vanguard Index Trust-500 Portfolio, boasts expenses of just 0.19 percent (compared to the expenses of the average stock fund, which in 1997 climbed to 1.22 percent). Of course, even small costs take their toll; that's why all index funds will slightly lag the index they're tracking.

Index funds can form part of a tax-smart strategy as well. Many actively managed investments are characterized by frequent buying and selling; unlike them, index funds typically just buy and hold the stocks in their portfolio. Such low turnover means index funds generate smaller capital gains—and therefore cost you less in taxes.

Who Should Invest

Investors who prefer to take a hands-off approach to investing and who are willing to accept market-average returns rather than face the possibility of

Vanguard:
King of the Index Funds

Vanguard founder John Bogle first enthused about indexing while writing his Princeton undergraduate thesis back in 1949. Putting his theories to the test twenty-seven years later, Bogle introduced the very first index fund, the flagship Vanguard Index Trust 500, to mixed reviews, particularly from his portfolio manager peers.

But the bull market of the 1990s gave Bogle the last laugh—and his company a stunning boost. Today, index funds are at the heart of Vanguard's philosophy, accounting for more than a third of the company's fund offerings and more than $100 billion in assets. Second only to Fidelity in size, Vanguard continues to surprise the industry. Always a proponent of low fees and bare-bones expenses, Vanguard slashed costs even further in 1996. With the average expense ratio of its equity and bond funds now just 0.29 percent, Vanguard reigns as the lowest-cost fund provider in the business.

Vanguard investors can find unbiased information about the company and its funds in the monthly newsletter *Independent Adviser for Vanguard Investors,* available by calling 800-211-7641.

Vanguard Funds
800-662-7447
www.vanguard.com

market beating ones. Index fund investors should take a long-term view in order to ride out the inevitable market dips; however, index funds can be a terrific low-cost way to add large-company exposure to a diversified portfolio.

Who Shouldn't Invest

Aggressive investors willing to take big chances for big returns (although, as we've seen, in a bull market index funds can keep up with—and even outrun—much more aggressive investments).

F.Y.I.

If you can't take it with you, can you at least make money on death? The Pauzé Tombstone Fund thinks so. This tiny fund invests in companies such as casket manufacturers and makers of granite memorial stones. Launched in 1997, the Tombstone Fund is finding death unforgiving. At the end of its first year, it trailed the S&P 500 by more than 38 percent.

Index Fund Opportunities

When it comes to index funds, costs really do make all the difference. While the following funds have all delivered attractive returns during the recent bull market, those with the lowest expenses—the Vanguard and Fidelity funds—have an edge in performance:

• **BT Investment Equity 500 Index Fund**
Minimum initial investment: $2,500; expense ratio: 0.25 percent. (800-730-1313)

• **Dreyfus S&P 500 Index Fund**
Minimum initial investment: $2,500; expense ratio: 0.50 percent; fund expenses have been capped—at least temporarily—by the fund company. (800-645-6561)

• **Fidelity Spartan Market Index Fund**
Minimum initial investment: $2,500; expense ratio: 0.19 percent; fund expenses have been capped—at least temporarily—by the fund company. (800-544-8888)

• **Schwab 1000 Fund**
Minimum initial investment: $1,000; expense ratio: 0.46 percent. (800-435-4000)

• **T. Rowe Price Equity Index Fund**
Minimum initial investment: $2,500; expense ratio: 0.40 percent. (800-638-5660)

• **Vanguard Index Trust-500 Portfolio**
Minimum initial investment: $3,000; expense ratio: 0.19 percent.(800-662-7447)

Specialty or Sector Funds

The grab-bag category of specialty funds encompasses a wide array of often unusual investments. Specialty funds can concentrate on a specific industry (like technology), a specific market segment (like gold or precious metals), or even on a specific cause (like many socially responsible investments).

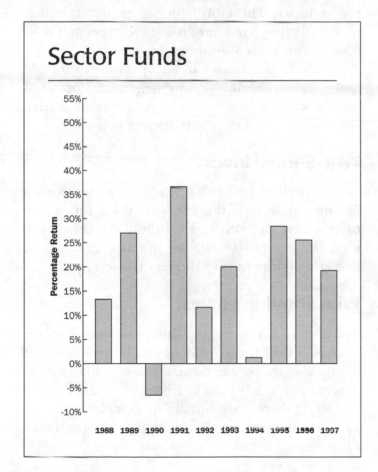

Sector Funds

Source: Kanon Bloch Carré

Not surprisingly, the performance of these funds is as varied as their objectives; while any might be an interesting addition to an already diversified portfolio, none should be a core holding.

That said, there can be much worth in many specialty funds. Sector funds, in particular, have generated tremendous gains—for those who choose the right sector at the right moment. Because they concentrate on one particular industry, including anything from financial stocks to biotechnology companies, sector funds forgo the broad diversification that characterizes the rest of the industry. Therefore, they're generally much more volatile—some might even say speculative—investments than most mutual funds.

Some sector funds can also provide a valuable hedge against high inflation; historically, precious metals, utilities, and natural resources stocks have performed well during inflationary periods.

Who Should Invest

Long-term investors with already diversified portfolios may appreciate the exposure these funds give to new and potentially rewarding markets. However, these funds should be monitored carefully, and bought into only by the very risk-tolerant.

Who Shouldn't Invest

Risk-averse investors or those with short-term goals will find the volatility of these funds rough going. For every spectacular run-up (like the 45 percent gains delivered by financial services stocks in 1997), there's an equally spectacular fall (the 42 percent decline suffered by natural resources funds the same year).

Socially Responsible Funds

Funds with a social conscience are a slightly different animal, guided by ethical instincts rather than purely financial ones. These funds—there are now more than forty—invest in the stocks of "responsible" companies. Although the definition of "responsible" may depend on the fund provider

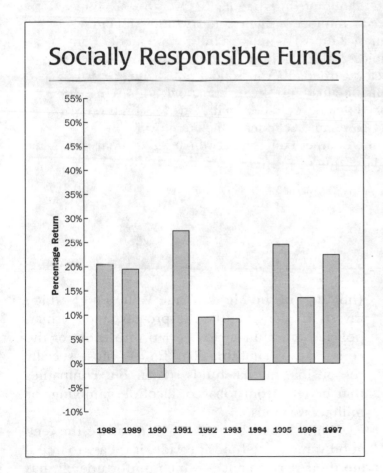

Socially Responsible Funds

Source: Kanon Bloch Carré

Scudder:
Investing with an International Flavor

Although eclipsed by its more marketing-oriented competitors, Boston-based Scudder Funds can lay claim to at least two financial milestones. In 1928, the company developed America's first no-load mutual fund; 25 years later, they launched the first international fund.

And it's in the international arena that Scudder still shines. Although domestically, Scudder is considered rather conservative (Scudder Kemper Investments, the company's investment advisor, also manages the AARP family of funds), they've continued to innovate internationally. Over the past fifteen years, Scudder has introduced a number of single country funds (including the first Korea and Latin America funds) as well as a full complement of other international and global choices. Although rarely at the very top of their class, these funds are generally well-regarded, offering solid if not sizzling returns.

Scudder—home of the first no-load investment—made headlines in 1998, when the company announced that it would begin charging fees on two of its funds. The Scudder Classic Growth and Scudder Value Funds will now be offered exclusively through the Kemper Fund group, which sells primarily through brokers and financial planners.

Scudder Funds
800-728-3337
www.scudder.com

(holdings of the Meyers Pride Value Fund, which invests in companies with pro-gay and -lesbian policies, are unlikely to overlap with those of the conservative Timothy Plan fund), most socially responsible mutual funds screen out companies that benefit from tobacco, alcohol, gambling, or military weapons.

While it may be difficult to measure the feel-good value these funds provide, it is easy to evaluate their performance—which, unfortunately, has been decidedly mixed. Worse still, many of these funds have hefty expense ratios, well above the industry average. However, the field is young; as funds gain investors and track records, expect their costs to drop and returns to increase.

Who Should Invest

Investors for whom moral concerns weigh at least as heavily as financial ones. While some socially responsible funds have performed quite well— both the Domini Social Equity Fund and the Ariel Appreciation Fund actually beat the market in 1997—the category as a whole has underperformed the majority of its stock fund peers.

Who Shouldn't Invest

Investors most concerned with financial performance, or those with only one or two holdings in their portfolio.

International Funds

International investors have had a rough ride recently. Japan's ongoing woes, Mexico's devaluation, and the Asian "flu" of 1997–98 have rocked both emerging and developed markets. But despite these well-publicized events, international funds are still providing the "world of opportunity" touted by fund company literature. In fact, despite the turmoil caused by the Asian currency crisis (which caused historic drops in the U.S., Hong Kong, and Brazilian markets, among others), funds that invested in European or Latin American stocks ended 1997 on quite an up note:

Rating the Ratings I

Feeling overwhelmed by the sheer number of mutual funds? An entire industry of ratings services and newsletters has now sprung up to help you make sense of the mutual fund world. Over the next few chapters, we'll take a look at some of the best resources now available.

Morningstar Mutual Funds
225 West Wacker Drive
Chicago, IL 60606
800-735-0700
www.morningstar.net

Chicago-based Morningstar is one of the best-known fund-rating services. Their in-depth reports are concisely written, putting a tremendous amount of statistical detail in reader-friendly terms. And Morningstar's analysts don't pull punches; they offer objective reviews of more than 1,600 funds. Subscriptions can be pricey; a three-month trial costs $55 and a full year of reports is $425. Morningstar also publishes a monthly newsletter, *The Morningstar Investor,* which can be a more cost-effective alternative.

Morningstar's web site is one of the more appealing on the Internet, and can provide a fast update on fund performance as well as general information.

European funds delivered gains of more than 16 percent and Latin American funds enjoyed returns of more than 25 percent.

By investing in companies located outside the United States, international funds can offer an added level of diversification to any portfolio. The idea is that markets don't move in tandem; what may affect the United States has less impact on Germany, and vice versa. Not only can international funds provide returns when the overseas markets are doing well but, perhaps more important, they can cushion your portfolio when the U.S. market stumbles.

Of course, investing in international funds does come with its own special risks. As we've seen recently, political and economic instability, particularly in emerging markets like Asia, Eastern Europe, and Latin America, are factors that need to be considered before you commit to these often very volatile investments.

And don't forget about currency risks. For international tourists, a strong U.S. dollar means they suddenly get much more for their travel money. However, quite the opposite happens to international investors. Their foreign-denominated

F.Y.I.

Global funds are often lumped together with international funds. However, global funds can invest in U.S. companies as well as those overseas; this means there's a limit on the amount of diversification such funds can really offer.

International Funds

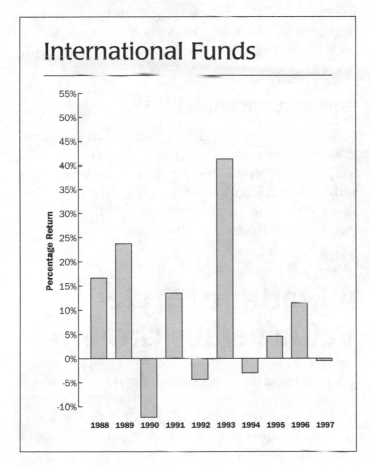

Source: Kanon Bloch Carré

gains can erode quite dramatically against a strengthening U.S. currency.

To reduce the risks of international investing, most financial experts advise holding these securities for at least three to five years. By giving yourself—and your investments—time to recover, you can better weather the short-term fluctuations that are almost guaranteed when investing in international markets.

Who Should Invest

All but the most risk-averse investors would benefit from the diversification offered by international funds. But it's important to maintain a long-term perspective; volatility is a given with these investments.

Who Shouldn't Invest:

Investors who blanch at a 5 percent drop in the value of their portfolio will be too uncomfortable with the 20 percent or 30 percent swings likely with emerging-market funds. And investors with short-term goals won't have enough time to ride out the inevitable market fluctuations.

A Matter of Style: Value versus Growth

These broad guidelines obviously allow for a lot of leeway. In fact, investors have complained for years that funds that seem to fall into the same general category invest and perform in remarkably different ways.

Because of this, many financial writers and ratings services have begun to look more closely at investing style. Style has more to do with how a fund invests than with what it hopes to achieve. While all aggressive growth funds aim for maximum capital appreciation, some may do so by concentrating on bargain stocks (*value investing*) while others look to find the fastest-growing companies (*growth investing*). Still other funds blend both techniques.

Size is an issue as well. Some fund managers invest only in large companies; others prefer the most micro of micro-caps. No one style is necessarily better than any other. But it has been shown that different markets favor different styles. For example, value-oriented large company funds (which tend to be more conservative) often do well during bearish markets, while funds that invest in small growth stocks often excel in boom times. Rather than trying to second-guess the market to determine which style is likely to do best, most financial advisers recommend that you open your portfolio to both kinds of investments, or else split the difference and find an appealing "blend" fund that invests in mid-size or mid-cap stocks.

THE BOTTOM LINE

Averaging annual returns of more than 10.5 percent over the last seventy years, stocks and stock funds can deliver the growth potential you need to beat inflation and achieve your financial goals. That's why they belong in even the most conservative portfolios.

But higher returns do come at a price: higher risk. Stock fund investors would be wise to take a longer-term perspective and expect inevitable—and at times, dramatic—fluctuations in fund performance.

Bond and Money Market Funds

Stocks may grab the headlines, but it's actually the bond market that moves the financial world. Many investors are surprised to discover that the total value of the U.S. bond market dwarfs that of the stock market; in fact, according to the Bond Market Association, more than $305 *billion* worth of bonds is traded every day.

As we've said before, a bond is essentially a loan. By investing in bonds, you're actually lending money to the bond issuer, typically a corporation, a government, or a government agency. In return, the issuer agrees to return your initial investment, called the principal, on a specific maturity date, and to pay you a fixed rate of interest at regular intervals until this time.

A bond's predictability is one of its chief attractions. Because it provides a regular stream of interest payments, many investors rely on bonds or bond funds to supplement their current income.

Bonds are also relatively stable investments, at least in comparison with stocks. Although they've certainly had their own ups and downs—just ask investors who experienced the wild ride caused by the interest rate hikes of 1994—bonds are typically less volatile than equities. More important, since they react differently to economic forces, often moving upward on the same news that can send stocks tumbling down, diversifying with bonds can help smooth out the overall performance of your portfolio.

Are Bond Funds Right for You?

While it's common for investors to own shares of individual stocks, it's much less likely that they'll own individual bonds. With typical initial investments of $10,000 or more, many bonds, particularly corporate issues, are just too expensive for the small investor. And, of course, that amount buys you only a single—very undiversified—investment.

That's why many people prefer bond mutual funds. Because bond funds invest in a large portfolio of different issues, they can offer more diversification at a much more affordable price. Another advantage is that bond funds usually pay income on a monthly basis, rather than annually or semi-annually as individual bonds do.

But while bond funds may be more appealing to smaller investors than the individual securities, they're still much less popular than their stock fund peers. According to figures compiled by the Investment Company Institute, more than $231 billion poured into stock funds in 1997, more than five times the amount invested in bond funds that same year.

Certainly, the bull market of the 1990s has had a lot to do with the decline in bond fund assets. Lacking the growth potential of stock funds, bond funds have delivered decent but far from spectacular returns for the past decade. While stock funds were averaging 16 percent gains each year, bond funds delivered just half that performance, averaging just over 8 percent returns since 1987.

But their lack of pizzazz shouldn't keep bond funds out of your portfolio. In fact, for some

SMART DEFINITION

Yield
"Yield" is the amount of income a bond generates annually, expressed as a percentage of its share price. For example, a $1,000 investment in a bond fund that pays $60 a year in dividend income provides a 6 percent yield.

There are many ways to measure bond yield; perhaps the most useful is current yield (also known as SEC yield). This measures the income earned over the most recent thirty-day period and best reflects current market values.

investors, bond funds may actually be a much more appropriate investment than many stock funds.

• **Do you need to earn income?** There's a reason bonds are often called fixed-income investments. The dependable stream of monthly interest payments provided by bond funds can help you pay your day-to-day living expenses.

• **Do you have short-term goals?** If you'll need your money within a few years, you may be better off buying a bond fund, which can better preserve your investment, than risking the fluctuations of the stock market.

• **Do you need tax-exempt income?** Municipal bond funds pay dividends that are exempt from federal taxes and, in some cases, state and local taxes as well—a tremendous advantage for income investors in higher tax brackets.

• **Are you concerned about market volatility?** Historically, bonds react much less violently to short-term market movements than stocks do. In fact, during the market correction of October 1997, bonds barely budged when stocks lost 7 percent of their value.

Don't Forget about Risk—Even with Bond Funds

Bond fund advertisements may lull you into thinking that these relatively conservative investments are in fact risk-free. But in actuality, all bond funds—even those guaranteed by the U.S. government—carry more risks than many investors may expect.

Dreyfus: Will the Lion Roar Again?

One of the best-known names in the financial world, Dreyfus has had more than its fair share of stumbles in recent years. Having pioneered the money market fund in the early 1970s, Dreyfus seemed to lose momentum for much of the 1990s. A cautious, cash-heavy strategy hurt the firm once the bull market took off. While many of its competitors grew fat with customer assets, Dreyfus instead became a takeover target. In 1995, the company was bought by Pittsburgh-based Mellon Bank.

But the Mellon purchase appears to have pumped new blood into the tired lion. Although Dreyfus is still best known for their fixed-income investments (which represent more than 75% of the company's fund choices), a number of new equity funds have roared to near the top of the performance charts. Of course, it may still be too soon to tell if the recovery is a permanent one or a brief respite. But with nearly 200 mutual funds to choose from (second only to giant Fidelity), Dreyfus certainly deserves at least a second look.

Dreyfus
(800-645-6561)
www.dreyfus.com

SMART MONEY

Interest rate risk is a concern even for professional investors. "As fund managers, we can moderate interest rate risk by changing the mix of bonds in our portfolio," says Brad Tank, director of Fixed Income at Strong Funds. "If we're being defensive on interest rates, we'll sell longer-term securities and buy shorter-term ones to bring down the average maturity of the fund—and vice versa.

"An individual investor can do the same thing. We see fund buyers move from short funds to intermediate funds, intermediate funds back to short funds all the time. But to get less rate sensitivity, they should focus on funds that always maintain a short average maturity."

Bond prices are inversely affected by interest rate changes. When interest rates rise, bond prices will drop; when rates fall, bond prices increase. This is *interest rate risk*, and the reason behind it is simple. Let's say you own a $1,000 bond paying 6 percent interest. At the end of the year, you've earned $60 in income. Interest rates then rise to 7 percent. For that same $1,000, an investor can now purchase a new bond that earns $70 a year. Not surprisingly, very few buyers want to pay full price for a lower-yielding issue. So the value of your investment will drop, from $1,000 to somewhere around $890.

Fortunately for bondholders, the opposite happens as well. Let's say interest rates suddenly fall to 5 percent. Your now better-yielding bond suddenly becomes much more appealing to other investors, and can command a higher price than you paid.

Obviously, interest rates will fluctuate over time, as will the value of your bond or bond fund. But chances are that rates won't change as dramatically in a year as they could over twenty or thirty. That's why the prices of shorter-term bonds (those that will be repaid in under five years) are less sensitive to interest rate changes than prices of bonds with longer maturities, and vice versa. Because of the greater risks involved with long-term bonds, issuers generally have to offer a higher yield to attract investors to these more volatile securities.

The quality of the bond and its issuer will also affect the amount you'll earn—and the risks you take. Remember that a bond is simply an IOU, a promise that your loan will be repaid. The more trustworthy the borrower, the more likely it is to repay your interest and principal. The less trustworthy the borrower, the more likely it is to default on the loan. This is known as *credit risk*; not surprisingly, the more risk you take on, the better the potential payoff.

As a rule, the higher the credit quality of the bond (or the creditworthiness of the issuer), the lower its yield. Conversely, the lower the credit quality, the higher the yield. Fortunately, the credit quality of most bonds is regularly evaluated by national rating services like Moody's and Standard & Poor's. Not surprisingly, the U.S. government is exceptionally creditworthy (paying off debt obligations is where much of our tax money goes). Top corporations are also generally reliable; bonds issued by a company like IBM, for example, are likely to be as safe from default as a Treasury security. These are all considered investment-grade bonds.

At the other end of the spectrum are what are known as non-investment-grade bonds. You may know them by their more familiar name: junk bonds. Junk bonds are usually issued by small or financially troubled companies; however, junk bonds have been issued by struggling municipal governments as well.

The ABCs of Bond Ratings

Bonds are graded much like students: straight A's signify the highest-quality issues while D's denote problem children. Fortunately, it's relatively easy to determine the rating of any particular bond (some of the smallest issues may not be tracked).

Both Moody's Investors Service and Standard & Poor's publish ratings handbooks, which are typically available at the library. The companies use similar, although not identical, systems to evaluate securities:

Moody's	S&P's	Quality
Aaa	AAA	Highest quality
Aa	AA	High quality; low risk of default
A	A	High to medium quality
Baa–B	BBB	Medium quality; possibly unreliable over the long term
Ba–B	BB–B	Bonds with speculative element
Caa–C	CCC–C	Extremely speculative bonds; high danger of default
—	D	In default

Yield Isn't Everything

Be careful of funds that trumpet high yields; they may not be the best—or even the best-performing—investments. Yield essentially measures only the income the fund produces, not necessarily how the fund has performed as an investment.

For a more comprehensive gauge of performance, ask about the fund's total return. Total return takes into account both yield and any change in the value of the fund's shares. For example, a fund may boast a 6 percent yield, but thanks to interest rate changes, its share price has declined by 2 percent. Add those together, and the total return on your investment is just 4 percent.

While yields are always positive numbers (you always earn income, even if the price of the bond fund drops), a fund's total return can in fact dip into negative figures.

Total return is also a good measure of the fund's risk exposure. You'll find that comparable bond funds invest in many of the same securities, delivering basically the same performance. So in order to boost those investor-attracting yield figures, some bond fund managers will load up on lower-quality issues or buy bonds with longer maturities. Not surprisingly, these tactics leave the fund much more vulnerable to credit risk or interest rate risk.

A better way to enjoy higher effective yields is simply to look for funds with lower costs. Since fees and expenses directly cut into a fund's return, investments with lower operating costs can generally offer more attractive performance without taking on undue risks. According to Morningstar, the average expense ratio for bond funds is 1.05 percent; fortunately, there are quite a number of investments—including bond index funds and funds from penny-pinching families like Vanguard, Franklin Templeton, and USAA—that are substantially less expensive.

The Bond Fund Universe

Investors have fewer choices when it comes to bond funds than they do with stock funds. But don't worry: that still leaves you with more than 3,600 bond fund opportunities.

F.Y.I.

Short-term bonds have average maturities of less than three years.
Intermediate-term bonds have average maturities of three to ten years.
Long-term bonds have average maturities of ten years or longer.

Bond funds fall into five basic categories: U.S. government (or government agency) bond funds; corporate bond funds; high-yield bond funds; municipal bond funds; and international bond funds. These fund categories are then subdivided according to the average maturities of the bonds the fund holds. Most bond funds come in short-, intermediate-, and long-term varieties.

U.S. Government Bond Funds

"Neither a borrower nor a lender be" is obviously not a policy followed by the U.S. government, by far the nation's largest debtor. The government and its agencies issued more than $7.5 trillion worth of bonds in 1997 alone—all the more opportunity for safety-conscious investors.

But that government guarantee does come at a price; U.S. Treasury securities, the most secure of all debt instruments, offer among the lowest yields in the industry. However, since the interest paid is exempt from both state and local (although not federal) taxes, your actual returns may not be as low as they would seem at first glance.

Slightly higher yields (although no tax advantages) are available with funds that invest in securities issued by government agencies like the Government National Mortgage Association (better known as GNMA, or "Ginnie Mae") and the Federal National Mortgage Association (FNMA, or "Fannie Mae").

Ginnie Mae and Fannie Mae funds typically pay yields one-half to one percentage point higher than those of regular government bond funds; in return, however, these "mortgage-backed" funds are subject to *prepayment risk*. Prepayment risk usually goes hand in hand with a drop in interest rates; as rates fall, mortgage holders are more likely to refinance their loans. As the original mortgages are paid back, the funds then have to reinvest in new mortgages paying lower interest—and producing less income.

In fact, you may want to be more careful overall when investing in government agency bond funds; although they generally offer high credit

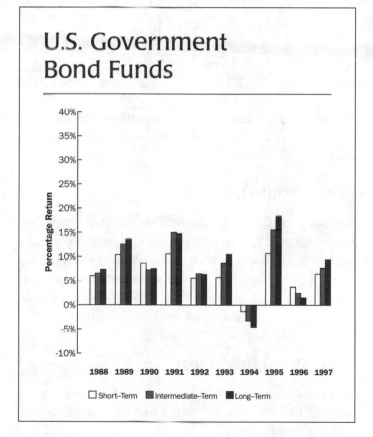

U.S. Government Bond Funds

Source: Kanon Bloch Carré

T. Rowe Price: Bonds and More

The first name that comes to mind when you think about bond funds is not T. Rowe Price, but perhaps it should be. In 1998, *Forbes* magazine gave Price's entire fixed-income category one of its highest overall ratings.

Founded in 1937, Price pioneered the idea of no-load mutual funds. More recently, this Baltimore-based fund family has built a reputation for providing solid investment offerings that deliver a good balance between risk and reward. Price is particularly strong when it comes to international investing, offering one of the few worthwhile global bond funds in the industry.

T. Rowe Price
800-638-5660
www.troweprice.com

quality, some may invest in more speculative securities that add additional—and often undisclosed—risk to your portfolio.

Who Should Invest

Treasury funds can provide regular monthly income, some tax advantages, and more safety than comparable bond investments. And these can be great investments for people with fast-approaching goals. Stick with short- or intermediate-term funds if you want to reduce your risks even further.

Who Shouldn't Invest

Investors who want better yields and are willing to assume higher risks may want to look elsewhere for bond diversification.

Corporate Bond Funds

Both large and small corporations often need to borrow money. They may be expanding, buying new equipment, trying out new markets, or even fending off a takeover attempt. One way they raise the needed cash is by issuing bonds.

Corporate bonds vary widely in quality, depending on the issuer. General corporate bond funds invest primarily in bonds rated as investment grade. (Funds that invest in lower-quality bonds will be discussed in the next section.) Because of the high quality of these issues, corpo-

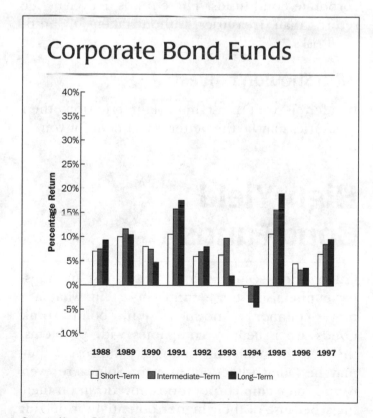

Corporate Bond Funds

Percentage Return

1988 1989 1990 1991 1992 1993 1994 1995 1996 1997

□ Short–Term ■ Intermediate–Term ■ Long–Term

Source: Kanon Bloch Carré

rate bond funds can offer investors better yields than government funds with only slightly more credit risk.

Like Treasuries, corporate bond funds come in a variety of maturities, from short-term to very long-term. By choosing to invest in funds with different terms, you can actually reduce your exposure to interest rate risk (remember, the longer the term, the greater the risk—and the greater your potential reward).

Who Should Invest

Investors interested in regular income may want to diversify their equity-heavy portfolios with some corporate bond funds. These funds deliver better returns than Treasuries, without taking on untoward risks.

Who Shouldn't Invest

If safety is your most important criterion, then Treasuries may be the better investment for you.

High-Yield Bond Funds

Calling these securities high-yield is just an industry euphemism; these funds invest in what are more commonly known as junk bonds. Junk bonds are issued by companies with problems: they may be small and financially unproven; they may be laden with debt already. Some are even former blue-chip corporations now down on their luck. Because of their higher potential for default

Smart Strategies: One Man's Junk

I'm extremely risk-averse, and I detest volatility," says Kentucky-based investor Gary Smith. But while Smith may call himself conservative, his strategy is anything but conventional. This investment writer loves junk bond funds—and has been remarkably successful with them.

"I first invested in junk in 1991, and made thirty-one percent," he says. "Over the last seven years, my returns have averaged around twenty percent annually." Gary considers junk funds such consistent performers, he actually uses them as an alternative to cash. "Junk is a great cushion," he says. "Even if their performance goes flat, they still throw off dividends of eight percent or nine percent."

Currently invested in the Strong High-Yield Fund, Gary dismisses junk's bad reputation. "For years, the newspapers have been saying that the junk bond market is poised for decline. Instead, junk funds have just been trending upward." In his experience, they're simply not as volatile as equities with similar yields. "Even in 1987, junk funds declined just two and a half percent, compared to the twenty-three-percent drop of the overall market. They're custom made for someone who doesn't like risk."

(these securities typically receive the lowest ratings from S&P or Moody's), junk bonds have to pay higher interest rates to attract investors.

Although not for the risk-averse, junk bond funds may not be as dangerous an investment as they sound. With the economy booming, the rate of default has dropped amazingly low (less than 0.1 percent of junk issues defaulted in 1997) while yields have zoomed into the double digits. In fact, most investors find that junk funds act much more like equities than like typical bonds: they perform remarkably well during bull markets and suffer during downturns. However, because they throw off income, they actually end up being less volatile than comparably risky stock funds over the long term.

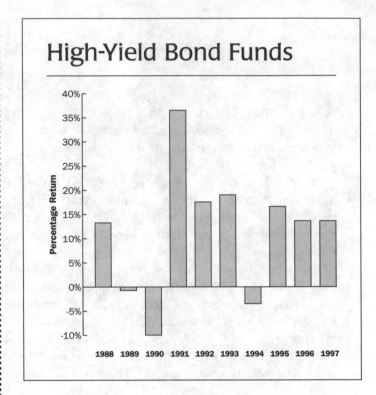

High-Yield Bond Funds

Source: Kanon Bloch Carré

Certainly, these investments aren't for every-one. If you want to test the high-yield waters, it may be best to look for an established fund with a proven track record.

Who Should Invest

Income investors who are willing to endure equity-style volatility for better returns.

Who Shouldn't Invest

High-yield funds are far too risky for those with short-term goals or weak stomachs. And because they perform much like equities, these funds may not provide enough diversification for a stock-heavy portfolio.

Municipal Bond Funds

The higher your tax bracket, the more you'll like municipal (or "muni") bonds. Issued by state and local governments, municipal bond funds pay interest that is typically exempt from federal taxes and, in many cases, state and city taxes as well.

Yields for municipal bond funds can appear lower than those of comparable investments. However, once you factor in their tax advantages, municipal bond funds often offer better returns than either taxable government or corporate funds—particularly for investors in the 28 percent or higher tax brackets.

Muni funds come in two varieties, each with different tax consequences. Some invest in securities from all over the United States; these pay income free from federal but not state or local taxes. (However, if the fund invests in bonds issued in the state where you live, you may be eligible for partial exemptions. Ask your tax adviser to be sure.)

Other municipal bond funds invest in bonds issued by a single state. Single-state municipal bond funds are subject to more risk because they're less geographically diversified (as anyone who held a California-only fund discovered when Orange County declared bankruptcy in 1994). Single-state munis do, however, offer "triple tax-free income"—that is, income exempt from federal, state, and local taxes—and this exemption

F.Y.I.

Unfortunately, only the interest you earn on tax-exempt municipal bonds is tax-free. Capital gains and investment gains are always taxable.

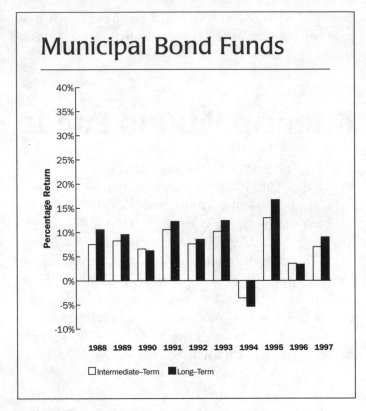

Municipal Bond Funds

Source: Kanon Bloch Carré

can help boost yields by as much as a percentage point.

Like their corporate counterparts, municipal bonds are rated for financial strength and creditworthiness. However, not all local governments come through with all A's. In fact, today, there's quite an active market for muni junk. Not surprisingly, municipal junk funds come with higher risks and correspondingly, higher potential rewards.

Who Should Invest

Affluent investors will most benefit from the tax-exempt income of muni funds. However, unless you live in a state with extremely high tax rates, you may want to avoid taking on the extra risks of a single-state fund.

Who Shouldn't Invest

Residents of states with low or nonexistent income taxes can probably find higher yields with other bond funds. These are also inappropriate investments for any tax-deferred account, like an IRA.

Taxable or Tax Exempt: Which Pays More?

Thanks to their tax benefits, tax-exempt funds often—but not always—end up yielding higher returns than comparable taxable investments:

Tax-Equivalent Yield

Tax-Free Yield	28% Tax Bracket	31% Tax Bracket	36% Tax Bracket	39.6% Tax Bracket
2%	2.78%	2.90%	3.13%	3.31%
3%	4.17	4.35	4.69	4.97
4%	5.56	5.80	6.25	6.62
5%	6.94	7.25	7.81	8.28
6%	8.33	8.70	9.38	9.93
7%	9.72	10.14	10.94	11.59

Money Funds Online

IBC Financial Data, one of the leading providers of money fund information, has created a web site to help individual investors find the money market fund that's best for them. IBC's Money Fund Selector helps you decide which features are most important to you, then provides an up-to-date list of all appropriate money fund investments. You can find the Money Fund Selector at www.ibcdata.com.

International Bond Funds

In theory, international bond funds are much like international stock funds; they can help diversify a U.S.-centric portfolio, providing the opportunity for international gains when the domestic market is on the decline. They also present similar risks of currency fluctuations and of political and economic instability.

In practice, however, international bond funds are unlikely to add any real benefit to an already diversified portfolio. Very few of these funds are truly international; most invest heavily in U.S. bonds as well. And historically, the returns provided haven't really justified the additional risks. If you do want an international bond fund, look for investments with proven track records and below-average expenses.

Who Should Invest

Longer-term investors looking for more diversification and willing to take on the risks of international funds.

Who Shouldn't Invest

Investors who already own a range of mutual funds, or those with solid exposure to U.S. bonds, will find that most international bond funds duplicate their current holdings.

Investing for Safety: Money Market Funds

In the industry, money market funds (or money funds) are known as cash equivalents. Highly liquid and exceptionally stable, they're almost like checking accounts—but with much better interest rates.

Money funds invest in short-term, high-quality debt obligations such as bank CDs, Treasury bills, and commercial paper (which is similar to corporate IOUs). There are also tax-exempt money funds, which invest in short-term state or local government debt. Typically, these types of funds are highly diversified, which helps reduce the already slim chance of default. However, it's important to remember that money funds are not backed by any federal deposit insurance and are not federally guaranteed.

That said, money funds are the most secure of mutual funds. In fact, they're managed to maintain a stable price of $1 per share; as a money fund earns interest, it will issue additional shares rather than allow the price to rise.

Many people use money market funds as a temporary parking place while they decide where to invest their cash; others use them in lieu of bank accounts because they can provide higher

F.Y.I.

Don't confuse money market *funds* with bank money market *accounts*. Although money market accounts are federally insured, they pay much lower interest rates— anywhere from one percent to three percent less.

interest with similar check-writing privileges (although you should make sure that your money market provider doesn't charge for these services).

Money funds have an important role to play in your portfolio, particularly if you're investing with very short-term goals. Just don't think of them as a primary investment vehicle. Although money funds pay more interest than the typical bank account, the earnings will hardly keep you ahead of inflation and certainly won't help you meet any of your more ambitious financial objectives. That's why almost all investment advisers recommend that you create a balanced portfolio, one that includes a healthy exposure to stocks for growth, bonds for income, and money funds for stability and easy liquidity. We'll talk more about portfolio building in chapter 4.

Choosing a Money Fund

There are three basic types of money funds: general-purpose funds, U.S. government funds, and tax-free funds.

General-purpose funds are fully taxable, but tend to pay the highest yields. U.S. government funds, which invest solely in Treasury obligations, are the safest (and consequently, lowest-yielding) option. However, some government money funds offer income exempt from state and local taxes, and that can help boost returns. Tax-free funds invest in short-term municipal debt and offer federally tax-free income. There are also single-state municipal money funds that provide residents with income exempt from state and local taxes as well.

Don't agonize over choosing a money fund. Once you decide whether you want taxable or tax-free income, these funds are basically all alike. To find a fund with the best yield and return potential, just look for the ones with the lowest expenses; typically, money fund expense ratios range from 0.5 percent to 0.7 percent of fund assets.

Many mutual fund companies and brokerage firms offer their own money funds. If yours does, you may just want to opt for convenience and keep all your investments in one place.

THE BOTTOM LINE

Too often overlooked, bond and money market funds have just as important a role in your portfolio as stock funds. Not only do these investments offer regular—and highly predictable—income payments, but they can also provide welcome stability during volatile market periods.

That doesn't mean that these investments are without risk. But by combining funds with different maturities and credit ratings, you can reduce your overall risk exposure and actually control your return to a great extent. In fact, investors are almost always better off when they look at their portfolio as a whole, rather than as a collection of single investments.

CHAPTER 4

Investing to Match Your Goals

THE KEYS

• First understand your own financial goals. Only then can you choose investments that really work for you.

• Be honest with yourself about the amount of risk you can *really* tolerate.

• Your time horizon is a key determinant to how you should invest.

• Too much of a good thing: why five or six funds are better than ten or twenty.

Every month, the financial magazines tout "the next best investments" or "the right funds to invest in now." But that doesn't mean that these are the best investments for *you*. In fact, often these funds are exactly the wrong ones to own—at least, given your own personal situation.

It's important to remember that every investor is different; everyone has unique needs and goals, even people in the same age group or income bracket. In fact, understanding who you are as an investor is the most important step you'll ever take. And finding the investments that meet your specific objectives will ultimately be much more important than simply looking for the best-performing fund.

Investor, Know Thyself

Too often, we plunge into the investing world without asking ourselves what we really want from our investments. Some of us may need to generate income to live on right now; others don't plan to touch their money for twenty or even forty years. Not surprisingly, these investors should have very different portfolios.

How you choose to invest will depend on a number of factors: your specific investing objectives; the amount of money you have to invest; when you expect to need your money; and your comfort with risk. Even your age is a consideration. Your answers to the following questions can help you determine what kind of investor you are and, more to the point, what types of mutual funds may be right for you.

What Are Your Specific Financial Goals?

You may want to buy a house in a year or two. Or send your child to an Ivy League university one day. Having a definite financial target in mind will help you figure out how aggressively you'll need to invest.

What Is Your Time Horizon?

Think about when you'll need your money. If you plan to tap into your assets next year, you'll want to be in very stable investments, like short-term bond or money funds. On the other hand, if you have ten years or so to ride out short-term market swings, you can take advantage of a stock fund's greater growth potential.

In fact, time is the most important consideration when it comes to choosing an investment: the longer your time frame, the more aggressive your investing strategy should be.

How Comfortable Are You with Risk?

Be honest with yourself: how much market volatility can you stomach? Can you tolerate losing 5 percent of your money? How about 10 percent? What if you looked at your $10,000 portfolio and it was worth just $7,500 after a one-day market drop?

Figuring out just how tolerant you are of market moves is crucial to choosing investments. If a

20 percent drop in the value of your portfolio would keep you awake at night, then aggressive stock or sector funds are certainly not for you. But that doesn't mean you should seek refuge in lower-risk/lower-yield Treasury securities either; as we'll see later in this chapter, balancing your investments—offsetting riskier stock funds with more stable bond funds, for example—will leave you feeling more comfortable with the market's inevitable volatility *and* help you achieve better returns overall.

The "Total Portfolio" Approach

When it comes to investing, the whole is often greater than the sum of its parts. Instead of viewing your portfolio as a collection of individual securities, think of how each investment works together—and how together they work toward your overall goal.

This "total portfolio" approach to investing is also known as *asset allocation*. It's simply a way of diversifying your investments to both maximize your return and minimize your overall risk. In previous chapters, we discussed how markets generally don't move in tandem. Over the years, large companies have performed well when small stocks have fallen, and international investments have often boomed even when the U.S. market stumbled. By exposing your portfolio to different investments (and even types of investments), you'll be better able to take advantage of any upturns, while protecting yourself from the full brunt of a market decline.

Take the Risk Quiz

1. Two months after you invest, your fund's value drops 20 percent. Assuming none of the fundamentals have changed, would you:

    a. Sell to avoid further loss?
    b. Do nothing and wait for the fund's price to bounce back?
    c. Buy more? (It was a good investment before; now it's cheap, too.)

2. What would you do if this fund were part of a portfolio being used to meet a goal that's five years away?

    a. I'd sell.
    b. I'd do nothing.
    c. I'd buy more.

3. What would you do if your goal were thirty years away?

    a. I'd sell.
    b. I'd do nothing.
    c. I'd buy more.

4. Retirement is only fifteen years away. Which would you rather do?

    a. Invest in a money fund, giving up the possibility of major gains but assuring the safety of your principal.
    b. Invest in a 50-50 mix of stock and bond funds, hoping to get some growth but also protecting yourself with steady income.
    c. Invest in aggressive growth funds, whose value will probably fluctuate significantly, but that have the potential for impressive gains by the time you retire.

5. You just won a big prize! But which one will you choose?

    a. $2,000 in cash
    b. A 50 percent chance to win $5,000
    c. A 20 percent chance to win $15,000

6. A good investment opportunity just came along, but you'll have to borrow money to get in. Would you take out a loan:

    a. Definitely not
    b. Perhaps
    c. Yes

Scoring your risk tolerance: Give yourself 0 points for every "a" answer, 1 point for every "b" answer, and 2 points for every "c" answer. Tally your points and compare:

Points	You may be a:
0 – 3	Conservative investor
4 – 8	Moderate investor
9 – 12	Aggressive investor

Source: Scudder Kemper Retirement Services

SMART MONEY

Financial experts like Maria Crawford Scott, editor of the *American Association of Individual Investors Journal*, believe that how you allocate your assets may be the most important decision you can make. "Assuming you have a diversified portfolio," she says, "deciding to go with x percent of stocks and x percent of bonds will have a bigger impact on your long-term rate of return than deciding to invest in any specific mutual fund.

"Remember, though, that your investment profile will change over time. Asset allocation should be a target; don't try to pinpoint exact percentages. It's much better to think of it as a guide that can keep your investments on track for the long term."

Asset allocation can be a time-consuming process, which is why it's one of an investor's least favorite tasks. But a 1991 study of performance conducted by money managers Gary L. Brinson, Brian Singer, and Gil Beebower found that how you allocate your assets among stocks, bonds, and cash investments actually has an enormous impact on your total gain—accounting for roughly 92 percent of your portfolio's performance. "Timing" the market to respond to changing conditions accounted for another 6 percent. And the actual funds selected? According to the authors, they accounted for just 2 percent of the typical investor's return.

Achieving Balance

The point of asset allocation is to create a portfolio that not only meets your investing goals but also leaves you feeling comfortable even when the market turns volatile. Ideally, you should be able to come up with an investment plan that works for the long term and allows you to ignore the market's inevitable short-term fluctuations.

You're aiming for overall balance—for example, offsetting the greater risks of stock funds with the more predictable moves of the bond market, or the better returns of small-company stocks with the stability of a money market investment. Each security you choose should complement—rather than duplicate—another, and work well with your current mix.

At the very least, you should diversify among the three major asset classes: stocks, bonds, and cash equivalents. To make the most of market

Rating the Ratings II: Fund Newsletters

Offering specific recommendations as well as model portfolios, mutual fund newsletters can provide a deeper layer of knowledge for the fund aficionado. But the detailed information these newsletters offer doesn't come cheap; annual subscriptions can range from $80 to $200. Over the years, the following fund newsletters have proven themselves worth the price:

• *No-Load Fund Analyst.* One of the most respected newsletters in the industry, this publication covers a relatively small number of funds. But detailed analysis, on-target reviews, and insightful articles make it well worth a look ($225 a year; $55 for a three-month trial subscription; 800-776-9555).

• *No-Load Fund Investor.* For nearly twenty years, editor Sheldon Jacobs has provided advice for the more novice reader. Covering nearly 800 funds—more than any other fund newsletter—Jacobs also offers specific portfolios built around Vanguard, T. Rowe Price, and Fidelity funds ($129 a year; 800-252-2042).

• *FundsNet Insight.* Editor Eric Kobren, who also publishes *Fidelity Insight,* tracks developments at the fund "supermarkets" run by Charles Schwab, Jack White, and Fidelity (see chapter 7 for more). Kobren's portfolios are well diversified, delivering typically less volatile returns ($177 per year; 800-444-6342).

Before you subscribe to any publication, ask for a sample issue. You may also want to check out the *Hulbert Financial Digest* (888-485-2378), which regularly evaluates the advice of some 160 investment letters.

growth, you'll probably also want to take advantage of subcategories like small-company and international stocks. And since investing styles can go in and out of favor, you may want to own both growth and value funds (or a blend fund) as well.

Don't worry if this sounds complicated; later in this chapter, we'll discuss sample portfolios as well as mutual funds that will do all the asset allocation work for you.

Rebalancing

Rebalancing simply means bringing your asset allocations back to your original percentages. This can be done either by selling some of the investments that have done very well or redirecting dividends or new money to the ones that have lagged. Because selling assets usually incurs taxable capital gains, most investment advisers recommend the second alternative. And this way, you'll also be able to take advantage of the laggards' relatively lower prices.

Keeping Your Mix in Proportion

Your asset mix is key to your success, so once you decide on a plan you're comfortable with, stick with it. However, investment gains (or losses) can change your percentages without your even realizing it. For example, thanks to the recent bull market, the stock portion of your portfolio may have grown substantially. Rather than 60 percent equities and 40 percent bonds, your portfolio now comprises 70 percent stocks and just 30 percent bonds. Although you may have enjoyed increased gains, you're now exposed to increased risks as well. That's why it makes sense to periodically rebalance your portfolio to keep your asset allocations in the right proportion and your risk firmly in hand.

Obviously, as you get closer to your investing goals, your needs and allocations will change. You'll want to move your assets from more volatile, growth-oriented vehicles into investments more appropriate for a shorter time frame. In fact, even the most aggressive investors should end up almost entirely in stable short-term bond and money funds by the time they need to tap into their assets.

Investing to Meet Your Goals

Unfortunately, there's no one-size-fits-all portfolio; in fact, even the investment plans that follow are meant simply as guides to help you create your own asset allocation strategy.

Although your time horizon is the most important factor to consider when allocating your assets, you should also take into account your own financial situation. How much money you have to invest, your tax circumstances, even the amount of time you plan to spend on your investments, should all be considered before you begin. In addition, most financial planners recommend that you set aside an emergency reserve that can pay for anywhere from two to six months' worth of living expenses. This money should be kept in very liquid assets; money market funds or extremely short-term bond funds are both appropriate.

Long-Term Goals: Investing for Retirement

This rather aggressive strategy is heavily weighted toward stocks in order to deliver maximum long-term growth. This type of portfolio is best suited for investors with goals that are more than ten years in the future. And it helps if you're not too risk-averse; you'll almost certainly have to ride out short-term market reversals on your way to these bigger gains.

Notice that while 80 percent of this portfolio is large company, international, and small-company funds. This allows you to maximize capital growth while reducing your exposure to any one market sector. Bond and money market investments are

The Rule of 100

Notice that each of these portfolios—even the most conservative—includes equity investments. That's because stocks and stock funds can help generate the growth you need to stay ahead of inflation.

Just how much of your money should be invested in stocks? Here's a short-cut to help you decide:

1. Subtract your age from 100.

2. Invest that percentage in stock funds.

3. Invest the rest in bond funds, minus 10 percent for money market funds.

simply used to diversify and add stability to your portfolio; if you feel comfortable with the added risk, you can certainly increase your equity holdings even further.

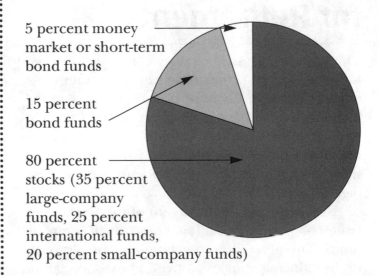

5 percent money market or short-term bond funds

15 percent bond funds

80 percent stocks (35 percent large-company funds, 25 percent international funds, 20 percent small-company funds)

New Opportunities for Retirement Investors

New tax legislation is rarely cause for celebration, but 1997's Taxpayer Relief Act actually did retirement investors a good turn. In addition to expanding the scope of the traditional individual retirement account (IRA), Congress also introduced an entirely new investment option: the Roth IRA.

Although funded with after-tax (and nondeductible) contributions, the Roth IRA offers the attractive possibility of completely tax-free withdrawals upon retirement—and potentially a much bigger nest egg.

Is the Roth right for you? A number of mutual fund companies, including T. Rowe Price (www.troweprice.com), INVESCO (www.invesco.com) and Strong (www.strong-funds.com), now offer online calculators to help you decide. However, it's always best to consult with your tax adviser about your own situation.

Intermediate-Term Goals: Investing for College

Do you see your eight-year-old in a Princeton sweatshirt? This portfolio is designed for investors with an eight- to ten-year time horizon. Stock funds still provide substantial capital growth, although since the intermediate-term investor has less time to recover from market setbacks, the proportion of money invested in equities is now much lower. Bond and money market funds again offer stability and capital preservation, as well as throwing off income to pay those first tuition bills. To protect yourself from interest rate changes, you may want to invest in bond funds with differing maturities, mixing shorter- and intermediate-term investments.

The equity portion of this portfolio is more heavily focused on larger (and often less volatile) companies, and less on more aggressive small-cap stocks. Index funds, which excel in tracking big-company performance, are often ideal investments for this type of strategy.

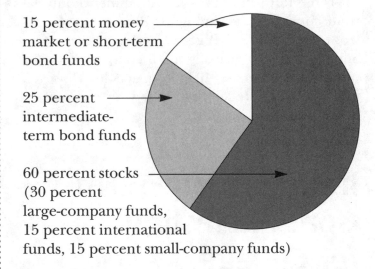

15 percent money market or short-term bond funds

25 percent intermediate-term bond funds

60 percent stocks (30 percent large-company funds, 15 percent international funds, 15 percent small-company funds)

Short-Term Goals: Investing for a House

Short-term investors face a dilemma: they still need to build their assets, but don't really have the time to risk a market downturn. This portfolio, designed for investors who'll need their money within three to five years, assures stability without sacrificing growth. The emphasis on bond and money market funds helps lock in gains; and by keeping a smaller proportion of the total investment in equity funds, you can grab bigger stock market returns without incurring huge risks.

However, if you're on the cautious side, you may want to reduce your stock exposure even further. Try substituting a growth-and-income fund for a stocks-only fund to take advantage of more stable—if less dramatic—returns.

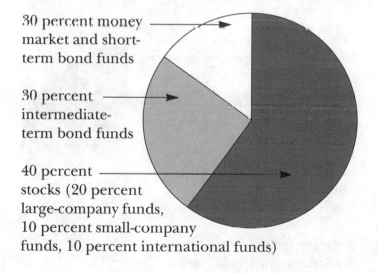

30 percent money market and short-term bond funds

30 percent intermediate-term bond funds

40 percent stocks (20 percent large-company funds, 10 percent small-company funds, 10 percent international funds)

"We started saving at conception," says Dick Vojvoda about his family's plans to pay for their daughters' college educations. Regular investing is key to the Vojvoda's strategy. "We earmark a certain amount of money every month, and we consider that untouchable," Dick says, "In fact, we invest in the college account before we make any other purchases."

With more than ten years to go, Dick and his wife Eve can afford to be aggressive; their portfolio includes small- and mid-cap value funds as well as some international choices. "Who's running the fund is what matters most to me," says Dick. "For example, if Helen Young Hayes [manager of two Janus Funds] were to leave, I would probably follow her to wherever she went next."

Immediate Goals: Investing for Current Income

If you need to live off the money generated by your investments, your strategy obviously changes. Income becomes the most important requirement, which is why this portfolio is so heavily weighted toward bond and cash investments. In fact, tax-conscious investors may want to consider tax-free municipal bond funds as well.

By keeping at least a portion in stock funds, however, this portfolio can continue to grow and stay ahead of inflation. Rather than investing in the more aggressive international or small-company stocks, this investor would do better to stick with a good large-company fund or a value-oriented investment.

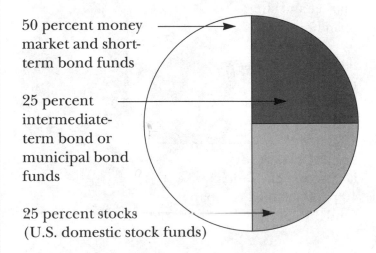

50 percent money market and short-term bond funds

25 percent intermediate-term bond or municipal bond funds

25 percent stocks (U.S. domestic stock funds)

Low-Maintenance Investing

Not everyone wants to build a portfolio from scratch; it can be time-consuming both to create and to monitor. Recognizing an opportunity, many companies have developed balanced-style funds that invest in different mixes of stocks, bonds, and cash. "Life-cycle funds," funds of funds and asset allocation funds all offer a diversified portfolio within a single, professionally managed investment.

In fact, for many investors, professional management will be the key incentive; the manager not only chooses the securities in the fund, but will also oversee and rebalance the portfolio as needed. Obviously, these funds can't meet your specific needs as precisely as those you choose yourself; however, they're often a convenient and low-cost alternative, particularly for busier or less experienced investors.

Life-Cycle Funds

As the name implies, life-cycle funds typically offer a choice of portfolios designed to fit the different stages of a person's life. Growth-oriented portfolios (which invest heavily in stocks) are aimed at longer-term investors, while income portfolios (emphasizing bonds or cash) are meant for investors with shorter time horizons. Dreyfus's Lifetime Portfolios and the Wells Fargo Stagecoach LifePath Funds (which actually shift your money for you as your goals approach) both offer well-regarded life-cycle fund choices.

Let the Pros Do It for You

The following funds can double as portfolios. While no substitute for doing your own asset allocation, they can save you substantial time and money.

Life-Cycle Funds

BT Investment Lifecycle Funds 800-730-1313

Dreyfus Lifetime Portfolio Funds 800-645-6561

T. Rowe Price Personal Strategy Funds 800-638-5660

Wells Fargo Stagecoach LifePath Funds 800-572-7797

Funds of Funds

Fidelity Freedom Funds 800-343-3548

Markman MultiFunds 800-707-2771

Charles Schwab Market Manager Portfolios 800-435-4000

T. Rowe Price Spectrum Funds 800-638-5660

Vanguard LifeStrategy Funds/Vanguard STAR Portfolio 800-662-7447

Asset Allocation Funds

American Century Strategic Allocation Funds 800-345-2021

Merriman Asset Allocation Funds 800-423-4893

Charles Schwab Market Track Portfolios 800-435-4000

Value Line Asset Allocation Fund 800-423-4893

Vanguard Asset Allocation Fund 800-662-7447

Funds of Funds

Some life-cycle funds are also funds of funds; instead of investing directly in securities like stocks or bonds, they invest in shares of stock or bond mutual funds. The appeal of these investments is simple: someone else is responsible for sorting through the nine thousand or so mutual fund choices now available. However, you should be aware that many funds of funds charge a double layer of fees: not only do you pay the expenses of the underlying investments, but you also pay management costs of the fund of funds itself. These charges can add up to surprisingly hefty amounts; for example, the Rightime Fund—one of the more established fund of funds—admits to investment expenses of more than 3% a year. Unfortunately, Rightime's performance far from justifies such enormous costs; the fund returned an abysmal -2.18% in 1997.

Two lower-cost (and typically better-performing) fund of fund alternatives are the T. Rowe Price Spectrum Funds and the Vanguard LifeStrategy Portfolios. These invest in funds offered by the sponsoring company, so you pay only the costs of the underlying securities and nothing more.

Asset Allocation Funds

Asset allocation funds have become increasingly popular in the last few years; according to Morningstar, there are now more than 160 choices. These funds double as portfolios; they spread their assets among stocks, bonds, and cash (and occasionally, other holdings like precious metals or natural resources), aiming for steady returns with relatively low risk.

Not all asset allocation funds are created equal, however. While some stick to a fixed allocation (for example, 50–60 percent stocks and 40–50 percent bonds), others can fluctuate much more widely, according to the portfolio manager's objective. The fund's prospectus should reveal the investing strategy the fund manager will pursue, or at least let you know how free a rein they're allowed.

How Many Funds Do You Really Need?

Don't confuse investing with collecting. While it may be tempting to own a host of mutual funds, in reality most investors are much better off with smaller portfolios. Even the most diversified plan shown here includes just five or six different investments (some financial planners recommend that you include both value- and growth-style funds as well, which would bring your total up to eight or nine *maximum*).

"Difference" is the key concept; all too often, investors chase performance, buying funds that made headlines or top ten lists regardless of whether these securities fit their needs or their existing portfolios. Owning ten funds that all invest in small-company stocks isn't diversification—it's just overkill. In fact, you may find that instead of being protected from market volatility, you're actually much more vulnerable to the swings of a single sector or even a single stock. To enjoy the true benefits of asset allocation, you need to invest in a mix of funds that complement one another, giving you sufficient exposure to different styles, sectors, countries, and asset classes, without needlessly overlapping.

And as many investors quickly find out, it's much easier to manage and monitor a smaller portfolio than a larger one, particularly if you invest with a number of different fund companies. Keeping track of multiple statements, prospectuses, and fund communications—not to mention tax documents—can overwhelm even the most interested investor.

There are certainly advantages to investing with multiple fund providers; however, sticking with a single fund family is often the easiest way to streamline your portfolio. A number of companies offer funds with very distinct strategies, and little repetition. For example, Franklin Templeton and Scudder Funds both pursue more style-specific approaches; their foreign funds typically concentrate on different countries or investing regions. American Century also provides a diverse lineup; their combination of aggressive stock funds and more conservative bond offerings is relatively unique within the industry.

As always, the best advice is to know just what you're buying. A fund's prospectus will explain the manager's investment approach, while annual and semi-annual reports should provide details about fund holdings. We'll talk more about these additional sources of information in chapter 6.

THE BOTTOM LINE

Rather than searching for the "best" fund, spend your time finding funds that are best for your needs. Build a portfolio of investments that work well together; a truly diversified plan will help you both maximize returns and minimize your exposure to risk.

But make sure diversification does not become *over*-diversification. For most investors, a portfolio of five or six funds is sufficient. You may even want to look into an asset allocation fund that does all the investing, monitoring, and rebalancing for you.

CHAPTER 5

Choosing a Mutual Fund

• Make sure a fund's goals match your own. Consider its investing objective, track record, costs, and risks.

• Don't overemphasize past performance. Today's highest fliers are often tomorrow's laggards.

• Is your fund *too* volatile for comfort? Determine how your investment performed on a risk-adjusted basis.

• It's also important to understand your fund's investment style.

• Not sure where to start? Help is available both online and on the newsstands.

U nderstanding your goals and planning an investing portfolio to match have an appealing—and often unheralded—side benefit: knowing *why* you're investing actually makes it much easier to figure out *what* to invest in.

Currently, there are more than 8,800 mutual funds available to individual investors (and given the fund industry's phenomenal rate of growth, that number will surely rise even higher by the time you read this book). It's absurd to think that anyone could possibly evaluate that many choices. And in reality, you'll never have to.

Easy Ways to Narrow the Field

Perhaps, like many of today's investors, you're saving for your retirement. Since your primary goal is long-term growth, stock funds are the obvious choice for you. So without doing any research whatsoever, you've immediately winnowed your playing field: rather than 8,000-plus funds, you need only consider the 4,900 equity funds now available.

Of course, 4,900 choices is still an overwhelming number. So concentrate on U.S.-based funds for right now. That cuts the pool nearly in half—to somewhere around 3,000. You'll probably want a proven investment, with at least a three-year—or, better yet, five-year—track record. That quickly eliminates another 2,500 possibilities. And certainly, you don't want to pay any unnecessary investing costs such as front- or back-end sales charges. That brings you down to just over 280 mutual fund choices—without having had to look at a magazine, read a prospectus, or check out a ratings service.

In fact, choosing a fund actually gets easier the more specific your criteria. Perhaps you only want to look at growth-and-income investments that have survived through both bull and bear markets (there are just thirty-three to choose from). Or you may be interested in an international fund with lower than average expenses (there are all of ten possibilities). So you can see that the mutual fund universe can actually be quite manageable—as long as you're looking for funds that rank high on *your* personal list, not some editor's top forty.

Getting Started: Performance Isn't Everything

That said, it's hard *not* to focus on a fund's performance. Touted in advertisements and quoted in magazine articles, performance figures are the numbers that grab headlines, making stars of portfolio managers—and, we hope, financial geniuses of the rest of us.

It's no surprise that everyone wants to ride a winner. But a fund's performance is simply a measure of what's happened in the past, not of what's going to happen in the future. There's a reason that every piece of literature from a mutual fund company carries the same disclaimer: "Past performance is no guarantee of future returns." In fact, short-term performance is frequently cited as one of the most un-

SMART MONEY

Why are there so many mutual funds? According to Russ Kinnel, Morningstar's equity fund editor, success begets excess: "Mutual funds have become an incredibly lucrative business. Even under-performing funds are wildly profitable. While there are plenty of quality choices, there are also a lot of companies that just can't resist coming out with gimmick invest-ments that no one really needs. That's one of the downsides to having so many funds."

F.Y.I.

Long-term fund performance figures enjoyed a major boost at the end of 1997. With the crash of '87 more than a decade away, many funds were finally able to drop that year's poor showing from their ten-year performance calculations.

reliable indicators of future success; independent studies by both Mark Hulbert of the *Hulbert Financial Digest* and Vanguard chairman John Bogle have shown that last year's best-performing fund is just as often the next year's laggard.

This doesn't mean that you shouldn't look at performance figures—they're often the only objective data you'll have. But remember that spectacular performance frequently comes at the price of high risk. And a stellar one-year return can mask quite a number of average or even below-average periods.

What to Look For

Rather than chasing today's high fliers, go for a fund with staying power. Consistent long-term performance is key, and a track record is vital; in fact, Morningstar, perhaps the premier mutual fund evaluation service, will not rate any fund with less than a three-year history.

Many advisers suggest you go back even further in time—if possible, back to the last market downturn. It's relatively easy for a stock fund to do well during a bull market; that makes it even more critical to find out how the fund fared when the market last turned bearish. While no one—least of all, a portfolio manager—can predict the future, past performance can provide some indication of how a fund might react to similar market conditions.

Performance information stretching back over the lifetime of a fund can generally be found in the prospectus. We'll talk more about prospectuses in chapter 6.

Measuring Performance

Average annual total return is generally considered the most accurate measure of a fund's performance. Taking into account the impact of distributions, dividends, interest payments, share price changes, fees, and expenses, total return figures can tell you how much a fund has actually gained or lost in value over a specific period.

Total return allows for much fairer comparisons between different funds within the same category. You can also use total return to compare a fund's performance with a relevant market benchmark, like the S&P 500 index for large-cap stocks or the Lehman Brothers indexes for bonds. While your fund doesn't have to beat the index, you do want to make sure that its performance is not out of line with broad market trends.

Performance results issued by fund companies, financial publications, and fund information services typically show average annual returns for one-, three-, five-, and ten-year periods.

Balancing Risk and Reward

Performance numbers alone tell only half the story; it's equally important to consider the riskiness of your investment. As we've discussed before, every investment involves some risk. Generally, the more risk you can tolerate, the greater your potential for gain (and, of course, the greater your potential for loss as well).

But just how much risk is acceptable for how much return? Is it worth taking on tremendous volatility—perhaps risking a 20 percent loss in the value of your investment—for a 20 percent gain? Or do you need the possibility to earn 30 percent

Risk-Adjusted Performance

You may have enjoyed terrific returns last year, but your fund bounced around like a roller coaster. Were the gains achieved at the expense of too much risk?

Risk-adjusted performance takes into account a fund's volatility as well as its return. Funds with spectacular performance numbers, like sector funds, can often rank very low on a risk-adjusted scale; they expose investors to a lot of volatility for the rewards they deliver.

or even 40 percent before that much risk seems worthwhile?

It's important to weigh the balance between risk and reward—and to be compensated accordingly; many investors are surprised when a fund with lower performance numbers turns out to be a better investment on the whole than a similar fund with higher gains but disproportionately higher risk. That's why many financial advisers recommend that you look at a fund's risk-adjusted performance rather than just straight returns—and that you carefully evaluate just how comfortable you are with a fund's volatility before you invest any money.

Evaluating Risk

To help mutual fund investors better evaluate risk, the Securities and Exchange Commission now requires fund companies to include standard mathematical risk measures when advertising fund performance. All but the most quantitative-minded investors will probably find these calculations too complicated for quick comparisons; however, these ratings—which can usually be found in fund prospectuses as well as in the fund rankings listed in popular personal-finance magazines—can at least help you judge the relative risk of different investments.

Beta

Beta measures how volatile a fund is compared to a standard market benchmark, like the Standard

& Poor's 500 index. By definition, the benchmark is given a beta of 1.0, so a stock fund with a beta of 1.1 would be expected to perform 10 percent better than the S&P 500 during up markets and 10 percent worse during downturns.

The more conservative a fund, the lower its beta. Equity funds with betas of 0.75, for example, would be expected to underperform the S&P 500 by 25 percent during bull markets, but to drop only three-fourths as much during bear markets.

Rating the Ratings III: Value Line

Value Line Mutual Fund Survey
220 East 42nd Street
New York, NY 10017
800-284-7607
www.valueline.com

Best known for its highly respected stock analysis, this sixty-seven-year-old company has now branched into the mutual fund world. The only real competitor to Morningstar, the Value Line Mutual Fund Survey is equally comprehensive if not quite as reader friendly. However, Value Line reports excel on tax issues and include valuable information about funds' performance during both bull and bear markets. Annual subscriptions cost $295, although a three-month trial is just $49.

The Value Line Mutual Fund Survey is also available on CD-ROM (for Windows only). In addition to the information included on the print reports, the software allows you to create and evaluate your own asset allocation plan using actual fund performance figures. The CD-ROM is updated on a monthly basis (but weekly updates can be downloaded via the Internet); an annual subscription costs $395.

Risky Business

Don't worry if beta and standard deviation seem too complicated. A simpler measure of risk (and one that takes your own tolerance for volatility into account) is often the most useful for investors. Take a look at a fund's worst-performing quarter or year. If you're uncomfortable with how much the fund dropped in that period (even if it fully recovered a few months later), it's probably not the right investment for you.

Standard Deviation

A more precise gauge of both up- and downside volatility than beta, standard deviation measures how much your fund will bounce around, so to speak, or how much it will deviate from its average return. By translating a fund's monthly gains over some specific period—typically, thirty-six months—into annual returns, an investor can compare how much the individual monthly performance varies from the average return for the entire time. The higher the standard deviation, the more volatile a fund's returns.

Average Maturity and Average Duration

Bond fund investors rely on these two measures to understand how the value of their investments will react to changes in interest rates. Average maturity is simply the average length of time until each bond held by the fund reaches maturity and is repaid. Generally, the longer the average maturity of the fund, the more volatile it is.

Average maturity can give you an approximate idea of how dramatic a bond fund's price fluctuations will be. But for a more precise measurement, most investors look at a fund's average duration. Average duration, which is measured in years, takes into account average maturity as well as early redemptions and interest payments, which can also affect the fund's value. Again, the higher the fund's duration, the more its value will fluctuate when interest rates rise or fall.

Understanding a Fund's Investment Strategy

Once you've narrowed your fund choices down to a manageable number, the real evaluation work begins. It's time to check under the hood, to find out how and in what your fund invests.

Does the fund favor small companies or large? Is the portfolio stocked with blue chip firms or is the manager more of a bargain hunter when it comes to picking stocks? Are there any international investments, or does the fund stick close to home? Asking questions such as these will help you ascertain the fund's investment strategy (or style), which is your best gauge of how the fund will perform and how much risk it will actually assume.

F.Y.I.

According to the Investment Company Institute, when evaluating an investment, 75 percent of investors consider a fund's performance, 69 percent review risk, 43 percent consider the fund's fees and expenses, and only 25 percent look into the portfolio manager's background.

Cynthia Liu, senior portfolio manager at Charles Schwab Investment Management, evaluates hundreds of securities for her four "funds of funds." So what does she look for? "We believe that consistency of the fund's investment style is the single most important factor determining good long-term performance. Managers who shift their style and chase market returns have to depend on luck to a large extent—and luck is unpredictable.

"A good starting point is to read whatever reports the fund company provides going back the last few years. Try to find interviews with fund managers that reveal how they go about picking stocks and how long they own their holdings. If you can, learn about a manager's decision-making process and investing philosophy."

Does Style Matter

A fund's style is characterized by both the size of the fund's holdings (whether it invests in large-, mid-, or small-cap stocks), and the fund manager's particular investment approach, either growth or value (or a blend of the two). Growth investors look for rapidly growing companies; they're willing to pay top dollar for stocks with above-average earnings potential. Value investors, not surprisingly, are more sensitive to costs; they focus on companies trading at prices below their true value.

Although neither approach is considered superior to the other, certain styles do perform better in certain markets. For example, growth funds often profit during boom times, while value funds typically do better during market declines or even recessions.

Don't Be Fooled by a Name

Unfortunately, a fund's investment style isn't always apparent from the fund's name or even its stated objective. In recent years, unsuspecting investors have found themselves in global funds masquerading as domestic stock funds (like the Fidelity Capital Appreciation Fund), in supposed growth funds that were heavily invested in Treasuries (Fidelity's Magellan Fund), and even in U.S. government funds that took remarkable risks with fund assets (the Paine Webber U.S. Government Income Fund). Not surprisingly, none of these funds delivered the performance that was expected; in fact, the Paine Webber fund suffered severe losses, which was quite a shock for shareholders counting on what is typically a conservative, low-risk investment.

Make sure you know what you're getting into. Read the fund's prospectus (which, admittedly, can allow for a lot of leeway, as Paine Webber investors painfully discovered), shareholder reports (which list all the securities the fund is invested in), and even the fund's Statement of Additional Information (which details fund operations and all expenses)—all of these publications must be made available to you by the fund company. Fund rating services like Morningstar and Value Line describe a fund's investing style and list its top ten holdings.

Who's in Charge of Your Money?

For many people, professional management is one of the key advantages of investing in a mutual fund; that makes it all the more important to

Taking Style to the Extreme

To the categories of growth and value managers, financial magazines have recently added *momentum* and *contrarian* investors as well. These actually aren't new styles, but rather extreme versions of existing approaches. Momentum managers—PBHG's Gary Pilgrim and Garrett Van Wagoner of the Van Wagoner Funds are probably the best-known examples—simply follow a very aggressive (and very price-insensitive) growth strategy, while contrarian investors—like Franklin Templeton's Michael Price—look for the most undervalued and out-of-favor stocks they can find.

Janus:
The Growth Stock Specialists

Denver-based Janus prides itself on being brash. Just take a look at the company's web site. Instead of the boilerplate language of other firms, Janus uses exhilarating (if sometimes confusing) snowboarding images to guide online investors through its site.

It's a fitting metaphor. Janus shareholders have enjoyed quite a run for most of the last ten years. One of the more aggressive investment firms in the industry, Janus specializes in growth stocks—which turned out to be the market's favorite securities for much of the 1990s.

The company fields an array of well-regarded stock funds, from the flagship Janus Fund (which, at $21 billion, accounts for more than half the firm's net assets) to the relatively new Janus Overseas Fund. However, as the funds have gained in popularity, their performance has stumbled—not surprising for a company that mainly looks for fast-growing opportunities. And Janus's heavy reliance on star managers can have unfortunate repercussions; one of their brightest lights, Tom Marsico, left to form his own investment firm in late 1997. So far the management change hasn't really affected his old fund, Janus Twenty, but investors would be wise to keep an eye on the fund's performance going forward.

Janus
800-525-3713
www.janus.com

know just who is handling your money. You should evaluate a fund manager (or team of managers) the same way you would any potential employee. You are well within your rights to ask how much experience a fund manager has and what other funds that person has managed. You should also find out whether the manager was responsible for the performance of the fund that you're interested in—or whether that record was due to someone else's skills.

You can usually find a manager's history in the fund prospectus. Unfortunately, these bios are often too brief to cover all the information you'll want to have before investing. For example, you should know whether your fund manager has managed through both bull and bear markets, and how his or her previous funds performed over various periods. If you're willing to do a bit of research, this information should be relatively easy to find; try Morningstar's web site or back issues of *Money*, *Kiplinger's Personal Finance*, and *Smart Money* magazines to start.

Does Fund Size Matter?

Is bigger always better, or can funds be victims of their own success? Rather than looking at the size of the fund, you may want to look at the size of the fund's holdings.

Funds that invest in medium- to large-size companies are typically better able to handle big growth spurts. Giants like Fidelity's Magellan ($64 billion in assets), American's Investment Company of America ($40 billion in assets), Vanguard's Windsor II ($24 billion in assets), and the Janus Growth Fund ($20 billion in assets) belie the myth that the larger the fund, the less nimble—and thus less successful—it will be. These megafunds have delivered average annual returns of more than 20 percent over the past five years.

However, funds that invest in small-company stocks frequently do stumble as their assets grow. Small-cap managers may have trouble identifying

F.Y.I.

Make sure you're paying costs that are not out of line for a fund's category. Higher-than-average expenses and good performance figures may mean you've found a top-notch fund manager—or may be a signal that the fund assumes much more risk than its peers.

enough worthwhile stocks to soak up the new cash that's poured in; frequently, these funds start investing in larger companies or taking bigger positions in the companies they already own. Both actions will affect fund performance.

In fact, concern about fund size will often lead a fund's management to close the fund, at least temporarily, to new investors. Large funds are only slightly less prone to fund closures than small ones are; in a headline-making move, behemoth Magellan finally closed its doors to new investors in mid-1997.

How to Invest in a Closed Fund

Managers may close a mutual fund for a multitude of reasons. They may fear that fund assets have grown too large to easily invest or that the market is too volatile for comfort. They may even find that the securities they typically buy are now too pricey thanks to a market runup.

But closing a fund to new investors doesn't necessarily mean the door is shut to new money. Additional fund shares are always available to existing shareholders and sometimes even to their relatives. According to Worth magazine, if you can prove that you're a spouse, sibling, parent, or child of a current investor, many supposedly closed funds—Janus Venture being just one example—will probably let you in.

Investing through your company-sponsored retirement plan is another way to enter through the back door. In fact, many analysts have criticized Fidelity for keeping Magellan open to 401(k) and pension investors who could add unchecked millions to the fund's already unwieldy asset base.

Transferring from a "sister" fund is a third method. If you're already "part of the family," most fund companies won't balk if you switch from one of its funds to another.

But just because you can find ways to invest in a closed fund doesn't mean that you should. Fund closure usually indicates that the fund company is concerned about future performance or, as in the case of many small cap stock funds, that current performance is already suffering due to huge asset flows.

Although some funds do close permanently (the $4.5 billion Sequoia Fund, for example, has not accepted new investors since 1982), most fund closings have proven only temporary. Typically, investors need to wait just a year or two before they can legitimately jump back on the bandwagon.

Comparing Fees and Expenses

How much are you willing to pay for your investment? Though all funds charge investors something for operating costs, some levy higher fees or run up bigger expenses. It's crucial that you know how much your fund will cost you—the more you have to pay for fund expenses, the lower your overall return. Fund costs come two ways: loads (a form of sales commission) and operating expenses.

STREET SMARTS

When Jim Keener bought his first mutual fund he took the advice of his Dean Witter broker and invested in Witter's Capital Growth Fund. When the fund's performance began to suffer, Jim realized he could do just as well investing on his own.

Today, Jim does his own research (supplementing Morningstar reports with *Money* magazine, *Barron's*, and the *Wall Street Journal*), looking for fund managers with consistent track records, low expenses, and small portfolios.

Although Jim now looks for less well known mutual funds, he recommends that novices begin investing with a larger fund family. "I've found that the bigger companies offer more choices and more support," he says. "Although I enjoy doing the research, it really is a lot more work to invest in a lot of different funds."

Seeing (Morning)stars

For good or ill, the Morningstar "star" rating has become shorthand for quality within the mutual fund industry. Morningstar itself considers its rating system a double-edged sword; although immensely popular with their readers, the company has found that investors tend to choose funds with higher ratings without necessarily understanding either what the stars mean or why the fund deserved them.

The rating simply compares a fund's risk-adjusted historical performance with those of similar funds; four- and five-star funds have consistently provided above-average risk-adjusted returns. However, it's important to remember that the stars have no predictive ability; in fact, the five-star PBHG Growth Fund was one of 1997's most disappointing performers.

Operating Expenses

Operating expenses include the fund's management and marketing fees, as well as costs for shareholder services like newsletters or check-writing privileges. These charges are reflected in the fund's operating expense ratio (summarized in the fund prospectus), and are already included in the cost of the fund. Typically, operating expense ratios average around 1.5 percent for most stock funds and 1.0 percent for most bond funds; costs will vary, however, depending on how much management is needed. Passively managed index funds are typically the cheapest investment, while research-intensive international funds tend to be on the more expensive side.

Loads

Loads are a different story; without too much effort, you can often avoid load charges altogether. (In fact, there are thousands of no-load funds now available, either directly from fund companies or through the mutual fund "supermarkets.") Loads are charged to compensate financial planners or brokers for selling particular funds; they range from as much as 8.5 percent of your investment to as little as 2 percent. Loads are typically assessed when you buy (a front-end load) or sell (a back-end load), and come right out of your investment dollars. For example, if you invest $1,000 in a fund with a 5 percent load, only $950 goes to work for you. We'll discuss fund loads and expenses in much more detail in the next chapter

Where to Get Help

Although quite a few investors still rely on financial planners to help them find suitable funds, many more have gone the do-it-yourself route. Choosing your own investments isn't difficult, but it can be confusing and time consuming. Fortunately, a wide range of resources is now available for both the novice and the more experienced investor. Magazines, newspapers, and web sites are all full of good (and sometimes not so good) information and advice.

On the Newsstand

Newspapers like the *Wall Street Journal, Barron's,* and *Investor's Business Daily* have all expanded their mutual fund coverage in recent years, while *Smart Money, Kiplinger's Personal Finance, Money, Worth,* and *Mutual Funds* magazines run detailed fund listings and related articles in almost every issue.

Remember, though, that editors need to create news stories; these financial publications tend to highlight the funds of the moment, which aren't necessarily the right funds for you.

Online

The Internet has opened the floodgates of financial information. Currently, there are more than five hundred sites targeted at mutual fund investors. However, you should be skeptical of what's out there; much of the information posted on the Web may be less than reliable.

Morningstar offers one of the best sites hands down, with top-notch articles, fund profiles, and investor forums. Other good places to find fund information, general research, and fund news include Yahoo Finance, Quicken, Mutual Funds Interactive (which is particularly good for fund manager interviews), and Charles Schwab's Mutual Fund OneSource Online. In addition, most fund companies have their own web sites, where you can at least get basic performance information and download fund prospectuses; Vanguard, T. Rowe Price, Fidelity, and Founders offer particularly informative sites.

Here is a list of top sites to check out. Some

even provide interactive assistance and can help you design an asset allocation plan or find funds that meet your specific criteria.

Online Publications

• Barron's: www.barrons.com

• Kiplinger's Personal Finance: www.kiplinger.com

• Mutual Funds Magazine: www.mfmag.com

• Smart Money: www.smartmoney.com

• Wall Street Journal Interactive: www.wsj.com

• Worth Online: www.worth.com

Fund Company and Broker Sites

• Fidelity: www.fidelity.com

• Founders: www.founders.com

• Charles Schwab Mutual Fund OneSource Online: www.schwab.com/funds

• T. Rowe Price: www.troweprice.com

• Vanguard: www.vanguard.com

Mutual Fund or General Investing Sites

• American Association of Individual Investors: www.aaii.org

• Morningstar: www.morningstar.net

• Mutual Fund Education Alliance: www.mfea.com

• Mutual Funds Interactive: www.brill.com

• Standard & Poor's Personal Wealth: www.personalwealth.com

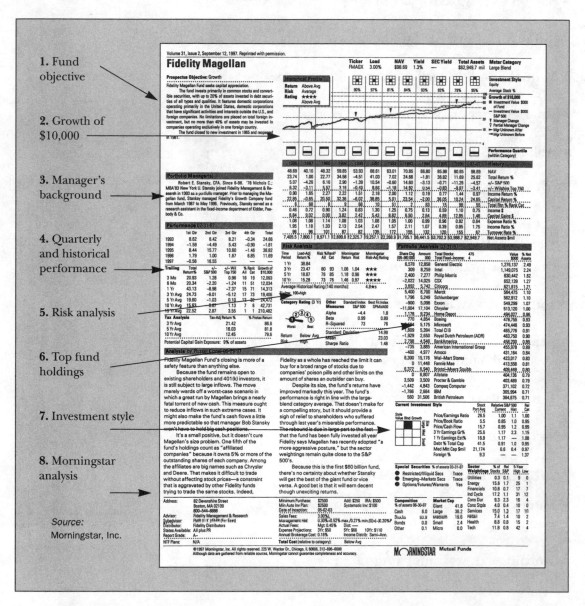

1. Fund objective

2. Growth of $10,000

3. Manager's background

4. Quarterly and historical performance

5. Risk analysis

6. Top fund holdings

7. Investment style

8. Morningstar analysis

Source: Morningstar, Inc.

- Quicken: www.quicken.com

- ValueLine: www.valueline.com

- Yahoo Finance: biz.yahoo.com

Fund Rating Services

We've already described Value Line and Morningstar, which are considered the two best evaluation services for mutual fund investors. Almost equally comprehensive, both Value Line and Morningstar reports include performance histories, manager profiles, and risk analysis, as well as an overall comparison of each fund with its peer group. Most individual investors will probably find Morningstar's reports easier to use. Value Line profiles tend to betray the company's institutional leanings.

Ratings services are really for serious fund investors; they're expensive, for one thing, and can overwhelm novices with much too much information. It's also remarkably easy to rely on the ratings given rather than exercise the proper due diligence yourself.

THE BOTTOM LINE

Make sure you know what you're getting before you invest in any mutual fund; understand the fund's investment objective and strategy, track record, risk level, and costs. Find out all you can about the portfolio manager's previous experience and his or her investment philosophy. Above all, the experts recommend that you look for consistency in both performance and investing style.

Thoroughly evaluating potential investments can be a time-consuming—although ultimately rewarding—process, but it doesn't have to be an overwhelming one. Fortunately, today's investors can rely on newspapers, magazines, rating services, and web sites for valuable investing information.

CHAPTER 6

....

The Fine Print

Fund performance may not be guaranteed, but fund expenses certainly are—which is why you should carefully consider costs before you choose any investment.

How Big a Bite over Time?

Fund expenses will have a direct impact on your returns. Although it may sound obvious that the lower a fund's costs, the better its investment performance, studies done by both Morningstar and the Vanguard Group have pointed out how significant this impact is. Suppose you invested $10,000 in three mutual funds. Each delivered an identical 10 percent annual return before expenses. Fund A was a relatively cheap investment, with a 0.35 percent expense ratio; Fund B had average costs of 1.5 percent; and Fund C was the most expensive, with annual charges of 3 percent.

Five years later, Fund A, with an actual return of 9.65 percent (10 percent minus 0.35 percent for expenses), has grown to $15,851. Fund B (actual return: 8.5 percent) has increased to $15,037. Fund C, however, trails the others. With an actual return after expenses of just 7 percent, Fund C has grown to only $14,026 over the five years. The difference becomes even more pronounced over longer periods: after fifteen years, your investment in Fund A will be worth over $12,000—39 percent—more than that in Fund C.

The Impact of Fund Fees

	Fund A	Fund B	Fund C
Expense Ratios	0.35%	1.5%	3.0%
Initial Investment	$10,000	$10,000	$10,000
After Year 1	$10,965	$10,850	$10,700
After Year 5	$15,851	$15,037	$14,026
After Year 10	$25,124	$22,610	$19,672
After Year 15	$39,823	$33,997	$27,590

Source: Morningstar, Inc. Chart assumes a $10,000 initial investment and 10 percent annual returns before expenses.

The Rising Cost of Investing

Not only do expenses have a long-term impact on your return, but expense ratios in general have been on the rise in recent years. Although some low-cost families—Vanguard is the typical example—charge as little as 0.30 percent of fund assets, the average mutual fund costs much more. Today's typical stock fund investor will pay annual fees as high as 1.73 percent of fund assets, up more than 37 percent since 1980, while a bond investor would pay an average of 1.05 percent.

Often a fund company will waive management fees or absorb fund expenses as a way to temporarily boost a fund's returns and attract new investors. But be wary; unless lower expenses are a permanent feature of a fund, your costs and fees may increase suddenly when the waiver ends, and then your returns will decrease accordingly.

Type of Fund	Average Annual Expense Ratio (%)
Aggressive Growth	1.73
Growth	1.45
Index	0.63
International Equity	1.86
Short-Term Bond	0.85
Long-Term Bond	1.036
High-Yield Bond	1.35

Source: CDA/Wiesenberger

The Basic Charges

All funds have operating expenses; they're simply the cost of doing business. Covering a myriad of charges—management and advisory fees, administrative costs, and marketing expenditures—operating expenses are typically expressed as a percentage of the fund's net assets, otherwise known as the expense ratio.

A fund's expense ratio is already reflected in the price you'll pay for your investment; it's not an additional charge. As we'll see later in this chapter, expense ratios (and all other investment costs) must be disclosed in the fund's prospectus.

Hidden Fees to Watch Out For

Not surprisingly, expenses are a sensitive subject for most fund companies. Criticized for rising fund costs (despite the economies of scale that should accompany their increasingly large asset bases), fund families are finding subtle ways to impose new fees, often hiding them amid marketing or distribution charges.

The most common of these is known as the 12b-1 fee, after an SEC ruling that allowed fund sponsors to pass along advertising and promotional costs to fund shareholders. 12b-1 fees normally run between 0.25 percent and 1.0 percent of annual fund assets (and are already included in the fund's operating expense ratio). While 0.25 percent or 1 percent may not sound like much, the 12b-1 fee has been a bonanza for fund companies, bringing in nearly $10 billion a year.

To be fair, there are often good reasons for some fund fees. To discourage excessive shareholder activity (for instance, short-term trading) that can increase a fund's costs, a fund may levy an additional redemption or exchange fee on top of the usual expenses. Typically, such transaction fees are assessed only when you sell fund shares or switch money between different funds within the same family. Frequently, redemption and exchange fees decrease the longer you hold your investment.

12b-1 Fees: Have You Seen Us on TV?

With nearly nine thousand mutual funds competing for your attention, fund companies have been pouring money into advertising. According to the newsletter *Fund Marketing Alert*, fund families spent more than $193 million on print and television advertising in 1997 alone.

Before you switch the channel or turn the page, you might want to appreciate those slick ads—after all, you paid for them with your 12b-1 fees. In fact, if you see a fund company advertising during your favorite shows, it may be a sign that its expenses are about to go up . . . again.

Reducing the Expense Bite

Expenses certainly aren't the whole story when it comes to investing; if your fund is delivering 30 percent returns, then sacrificing 2 percent or 3 percent to costs won't seem like very much. But if and when fund performance falters, you'll certainly feel that expense bite; these costs immediately reduce your gain.

Although the markets have been on a tear throughout the '90s, most investing experts expect much more moderate returns in the future. That's why it makes sense to look for value today—and cut your costs before they cut into your return.

1. Invest in funds with no 12b-1 fees and low ongoing expenses.

2. Avoid redemption fees or back-end loads by investing for the long term.

3. Purchase your fund directly from the fund company so there's no need to pay a broker or salesperson.

4. Buy index funds for the core of your portfolio. These passively managed investments have exceptionally low expense ratios.

5. Invest through your company's retirement program or a financial planner to take advantage of no-load Class D shares (which are typically available only to institutional investors).

Penny-Pinching Funds

With an average expense ratio of just 0.29 percent, Vanguard is by far the industry tightwad. However, quite a number of fund families have been able to keep their expenses under control, most notably American Century (average costs: 0.75 percent), T. Rowe Price (0.87 percent), and Neuberger & Berman (0.98 percent).

Industry spendthrifts, on the other hand, include Kaufmann (a whopping 1.93 percent average annual expense ratio), Pioneer (1.90 percent), GT Global (1.83 percent), and Oppenheimer (1.62 percent).

Paying Extra: Load Funds

We discussed load funds briefly in the last chapter; sold primarily through brokers, financial planners, and even insurance agents, load funds carry a onetime sales charge or commission to compensate the distributor.

Loads generally range from 2.0 percent to 5.75 percent, although they can legally go as high as 8.5 percent of your investment. They are typically assessed either when you buy (a front-end load) or sell (a back-end load) fund shares. A fund's load is not included in its purchase price, but, rather, is an additional charge.

Load funds are criticized for effectively reducing the amount you invest. Let's say, for example, that you plan to invest $10,000 in a fund that charges an up-front load of 5 percent. Of your money, $500 immediately goes to compensate whoever sold you the fund, leaving only $9,500 invested. So you'll need to earn 5.3 percent (or $500) in that first year just to break even.

However, there's no correlation between load and performance. According to Morningstar, funds that impose loads have not performed any better, on average, than funds that don't; in fact, after the sales charge is accounted for, load funds typically lag their cheaper counterparts.

But don't interpret this to mean that you should never buy a load fund. Today, more than 60 percent of all funds carry loads, including popular and well-performing investments like Fidelity's Magellan Fund or American's Investment Company of America. As long as you're getting sound

F.Y.I.

Retirement investors, take note: many fund companies, including Fidelity, will waive a fund's load if you're investing in a qualified retirement account like an IRA or 401(k) plan.

F.Y.I.

If you want investment guidance that doesn't steer you to load funds, look for a fee-based financial planner. For a referral, call the National Association of Personal Financial Advisors: (800) 366-2722.

advice and good service, there's nothing wrong with paying a load. But it's important to understand that you do have alternatives; later in this chapter, we'll discuss no-load funds as well.

Understanding Share Classes

Just to make things more confusing, load funds are often sold in different "classes" of shares, each with its own fees and expenses. It's not always obvious which share class is right for you; to make the most sensible decision, you'll need to consider both the amount of money you plan to invest and your time frame.

Class A Shares

This is simply another name for a fund with a front-end load. Buyers of Class A shares typically pay an initial sales load of 4 percent to 6 percent (generally this decreases as the amount you invest increases), but pay much lower annual expenses and marketing fees than buyers of either B or C shares.

Long-term investors may actually be best off with Class A shares; although you pay a higher price up front, you'll usually incur lower expenses over the life of your investment.

Class B Shares

Funds with back-end or deferred loads are called B shares; you're charged the fee only when you sell the fund. Back-end loads typically start at 5 percent and decrease gradually over six to eight years (in fact, once the back-end load disappears, the shares often convert to Class A).

At first glance, then, it would seem that Class B shares are the best option for most investors. However, owners of Class B shares usually pay higher-than-average annual expenses, which over time can result in lower returns than simply paying a onetime initial sales charge.

Class C Shares

These are also known as level-load funds. If you buy Class C shares, you're typically charged a flat 1 percent fee when you first invest, and then a similar (or level) amount each year in annual expenses and marketing fees. As they do with Class B shares, these ongoing charges may have a significant negative impact on overall returns.

Class D Shares

Purchase of these shares is usually limited to institutional shareholders (like investment advisers or corporate pension programs). Class D shares come with no load and no fees whatsoever—and not surprisingly, offer the best returns.

You may be eligible to invest in these no-load shares through your company's 401(k) retirement

SMART MONEY

Pay attention to the transaction costs incurred by a fund's portfolio manager, cautions John Woerth, a principal with the Vanguard Group: "An investor would be wise to look at a fund's portfolio turnover rate to get a sense of how often the fund buys and sells securities. High turnover not only reduces returns on an aggregate basis, but can also result in taxable capital gains that lower your investment returns even more.

So the impact is two fold: higher brokerage costs as well as the tax consequences of frequent selling activity."

F.Y.I.

Ongoing fund fees can take a real toll on your returns. Over time, a 12b-1 fee could actually cost you much more than a onetime sales load.

plan; however, as we'll see in the next section, there are plenty of other no-load funds already available to individual investors.

No-Load Funds

True to their name, no-load mutual funds charge no extra sales commissions. They're sold either by the fund company itself or through fund supermarkets like the ones run by Fidelity, Charles Schwab, and Jack White & Company (see chapter 7 for more information).

No-load funds have become increasingly popular in recent years; today, thousands are available. In fact, quite a number of well-respected fund companies specialize in no-loads: Scudder, Baron, Janus, Strong, American Century, and T. Rowe Price are just a few.

But while no-load funds may not carry obvious sales charges, that doesn't mean they're free of fees; in fact, over time, the distinction between "load" and "no-load" has become somewhat blurred. According to the SEC, no-load funds are allowed to levy certain charges that aren't related to the cost of investment management, in particular 12b-1 fees. However, a fund cannot legally call itself a no-load if it charges 12b-1 fees in excess of 0.25 percent, even if it has no other expenses.

The nonprofit American Association of Individual Investors (AAII) publishes an extensive listing of low-cost funds. Updated annually, the *Individual Investor's Guide to Low-Load Mutual Funds* costs $24.95 (it's free to AAII members). For a copy, call 800-428-2244 or order via their web site at www.aaii.com.

Load or No-Load: How Can You Tell?

The mutual fund listings in your daily newspaper will tell you whether a fund imposes any load or 12b-1 fees. Typically, no-load funds are highlighted with an "NL," while specific load percentages are included in a "sales load" or "sales charge" column.

Newspapers also employ an alphabet soup of ratings to explain specific fund fees. A "b" or "p" means the fund has a 12b-1 fee; a "d" or "r"

Franklin Templeton: Investing's Triple Threat

Once known solely for its bond funds, Franklin Templeton has been on a buying tear in recent years—and in the process has transformed itself into the industry's triple threat, offering a lineup of some of today's most respected fixed-income, international, and domestic equity investments.

With 1992's purchase of the much-admired Templeton group, the company acquired global depth as well as the services of star managers Mark Mobius and Mark Holowesko. Four years later, Franklin Templeton brought the popular Mutual Series funds, run by value investor extraordinaire Michael Price, into the fold.

Not surprisingly, this much investing talent costs: fund loads for the Franklin Templeton group range from 4 percent to more than 6 percent. But investors haven't seemed to mind. With more than $225 billion now under management, Franklin Templeton has grown into one of today's top five fund companies.

Franklin Templeton
800-372-6554
www.franklin-templeton.com

denotes a deferred sales charge or redemption fee; an "f" marks front-end-load funds; and an "m" or "t" indicates multiple expenses, usually both redemption and 12b-1 fees. We'll talk more about how to read a newspaper listing in chapter 8.

Required Reading: The Fund Prospectus

The fund prospectus contains valuable information about your investment. In addition to listing most of the fund's fees and expenses, the prospectus also outlines the fund's investment objective, its performance history, and its potential risks. You'll also find information about how to buy and sell fund shares.

Until recently, fund prospectuses have had a deservedly poor reputation. Filled with dense legalese and impenetrable financial jargon, prospectuses made for frustrating reading and were frequently ignored by investors. But thanks to an SEC ruling, fund prospectuses will be completely overhauled by December 1999. The new shareholder-friendly prospectuses must be written in plain English, using short sentences and everyday language, and organized in an easier-to-read format. In addition, technical information about the fund will be moved to other documents, so that investors can focus on the sections most relevant to their decision-making: investment goals and strategy, fund expenses, risk, and performance.

Specific guidelines and suggested language were still being determined at the time of this writing; however, the following example of a streamlined prospectus should be very similar to the final, SEC-approved version.

Section One: Fund Goals and Investment Strategy

The "goal" section of the prospectus will tell you what the fund seeks to achieve, whether that's growth, income, preservation of capital, international exposure, or something else. Don't be surprised if the fund's goals are stated rather broadly; funds typically prefer to give the fund manager substantial flexibility, rather than have to change the prospectus at a later date.

The prospectus's investment strategy section, on the other hand, will be much more detailed, spelling out how and in what securities the fund will invest. You'll often find specific asset percentages listed; for example, the prospectus for the State Street Emerging Growth Fund allows for 65 percent of fund assets to be invested in small, fast-growing (or "emerging") companies and 35 percent in other securities (which can include riskier international investments or derivatives).

This section should be a crucial one for all investors; if you feel uncomfortable because a fund manager has the option to invest in speculative securities or employ a potentially risky strategy, you may want to choose a different fund.

F.Y.I.

What are the "other" expenses often mentioned in a fund's prospectus? This charge covers such shareholder conveniences as newsletters, account statements, fund mailings, twenty-four-hour telephone service, and even the automatic reinvestment of dividends.

Section Two: Portfolio Risks

Ignorance isn't bliss when it comes to investing. To make sure you know exactly what you're getting into, the SEC has mandated that the risk section of the prospectus clearly explain what chances the fund manager is allowed to take with your money—and what can go wrong with his investment choices.

This section is something like a warning label for investors, and the language pulls few punches when it comes to outlining potential hazards. For example, emerging growth stocks, like those purchased by the State Street fund, are susceptible to "sudden, unpredictable drops in value and periods of lackluster performance."

Section Three: Investor Expenses

For the past few years, mutual funds have been required to display all expense information in an easy-to-read table. The new prospectuses will continue to include this feature; a number of funds have also begun highlighting specific expenses (like exchange or account maintenance fees) that were previously more hidden.

The first half of the fee table lists any transaction expenses, such as sales loads or redemption fees. The second half of the table includes all operating expenses on the part of the fund; management, marketing, and fund servicing fees must be clearly identified.

In addition, the prospectus must also include a hypothetical example showing the amount you would have paid in fees and expenses on a $1,000 investment earning a 5 percent rate of return. Expenses are calculated for one-, three-, five-, and ten-year periods to illustrate the effects of both up-front loads and ongoing fees.

	Class descriptions begin on page 12			
Shareholder Fees (% of offering price)[1]	Class A	Class B	Class C[2]	Class S[2]
Maximum front-end sales charge	4.50	0.00	0.00	0.00
Maximum deferred sales charge	0.00[3]	5.00	1.00	0.00
Annual Fund Expenses (% of average net assets)	Class A	Class B	Class C	Class S
Management fee	0.75	0.75	0.75	0.75
Marketing/service (12b-1) fees[4]	0.25	1.00	1.00	0.00
Other expenses, after voluntary reduction[5]	0.35	0.35	0.35	0.35
Total annual fund expenses, after voluntary reduction[5]	1.35	2.10	2.10	1.10
Year	Class A	Class B[7]	Class C[7]	Class S
1	$58	$71/$21	$31/$21	$11
3	$96	$96/$66	$66/$66	$35
5	$116	$133/$113	$113/$113	$61
10	$200	$224/$224	$243/$243	$134

Source: State Street Research and Management

Section Four: Financial Highlights

How has your investment performed over the past few years? The tables in the financial highlights section track changes in the fund's share price, total return, distributions, and asset growth.

You'll also find a listing for the portfolio's turnover rate. This indicates how frequently the fund manager buys and sells securities. Because

What Securities Does a Fund Own?

The annual or semi-annual report will list all fund holdings as of a specific date, including complicated assets like derivatives that aren't mentioned in the fund's prospectus. Knowing what a fund invests in can give you a better idea of the fund's volatility and potential performance.

each trade incurs brokerage commissions, high portfolio turnover can mean higher fund costs (as well as bigger tax consequences; for more information about taxes, see chapter 8).

Funds will also literally illustrate their performance. Many prospectuses already include graphs showing how a $10,000 investment would have fared over the years; others compare the fund's performance to a relevant benchmark index. In addition to these measures, the new prospectuses will also include a bar chart of ten-year annual returns as well as a description of the fund's best- and worst-performing quarters to give a better indication of fund volatility.

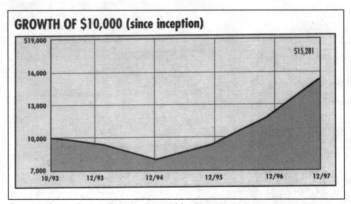

Source: State Street Research and Management

The Profile Prospectus

The typical prospectus easily runs to twenty or more pages, which is a tremendous amount of information even in the "plain English" version. To give investors another, more accessible option, the SEC recently allowed for the distribution of a more concise summary of relevant fund information. Running just three to six pages, the so-called profile prospectus includes the eleven items investors most need to know before making an investment decision:

• Fund goals or objectives

• Investment strategy

• Risks

• Investors for whom the fund would be most appropriate

• Fee and expense table

• Graphic depiction of fund performance over time

• Name and biography of the fund's investment adviser

• Fund-buying information, including initial investment minimums

• Fund-redemption information

• Dates of fund distributions

• Additional fund services

Because an investor can invest in a fund having been provided with nothing more than the profile prospectus, these summaries will likely be used in lieu of current fund advertisements and on fund company web sites. Investors who buy fund shares on the basis of a profile prospectus will receive the full version with their confirmation statements.

For More Information: Statements of Additional Information and Fund Reports

Either version of the prospectus should tell you most of what you'll want to know before investing; however, fund companies also make available other documents that reveal more facts and figures about your potential investment.

For example, a fund's Statement of Additional Information (SAI), which is also called Part B of the prospectus, explains fund operations, trading policies, and tax and accounting considerations in great (some might say excruciating) detail. Although not for the casual reader, the SAI is useful because it can provide additional information about fund expenses (including a breakdown of distribution fees) and portfolio turnover rate.

If you're interested in obtaining an SAI, you must specifically request one from your fund company; these reports aren't made available on a general basis.

Annual and semi-annual reports, on the other hand, are regularly mailed to fund shareholders. An annual report actually allows the fund to speak for itself; in addition to giving a performance update, it lists all the securities owned by the fund and usually includes commentary from the portfolio manager as well as the fund company's chairman.

Annual and semi-annual reports are more than just marketing literature; they should provide an honest assessment of both prevailing market conditions and your fund's response to them. You should find straightforward explanations of why your fund performed either poorly or well, and of the manager's expectations (and strategies) for the future.

THE BOTTOM LINE

Fund advertisements admonish you to read the prospectus carefully before investing. It's good advice—the prospectus includes important information which you should consider before you make any final decisions.

For example, you'll want to take a close look at a fund's expenses. Since these costs directly diminish fund returns, you'll want to minimize fees wherever possible.

It's also important to understand how and in what your fund invests. So, in addition to reading the prospectus, you may want to look at a fund's annual and semi-annual reports, as well as its Statement of Additional Information.

Buying a Mutual Fund

Today, it may be easier to purchase a mutual fund than it is to buy a postage stamp. Funds are now sold almost everywhere—through banks, brokerage firms, insurance agents, and affinity organizations like the AARP. Even the airlines have gotten into the act: American Airlines not only sponsors its own fund family, but actually distributes prospectuses to passengers in flight.

So what's the best way to buy funds? The answer will vary, depending on what you need as an investor. For example, you may want the advice and research that a full-commission broker can offer. Or you may prefer to do it yourself, and take advantage of the selection of funds available through many discount brokerage firms. Some people like investing online, while others value a one-on-one relationship.

Once you understand what's most important to you—whether that's convenience, price, selection, advice, or simply access to a particular fund—you'll find it much easier to decide how and where you should invest.

Buying Directly from a Fund Company

Most mutual funds are available right from the source: the fund company itself. Not surprisingly, dispensing with a middleman can often save you money. When you buy direct, you typically pay no sales commissions (although some funds, like Fidelity's Magellan, may levy marketing fees of as much as 3 percent). And as we saw in chapter 6, lower costs generally translate to higher actual returns.

To encourage the small investor, many no-load fund families have made it very easy to invest; calling a toll-free number and mailing a check is usually all that's required. And while you won't find much individualized assistance with your investment planning, fund companies have gotten much better about providing educational materials or even interactive help via the Internet. Founders Funds, for example, offers retirement and college planning calculators on their web site, at www.founders.com.

If you plan to invest in funds from only one company, buying direct is undoubtedly your best option. Certainly, many families—for example, Fidelity, Vanguard, and T. Rowe Price—provide more than enough fund choices to create a well-diversified portfolio with just their own offerings. However, if you do plan to invest in funds from different companies, you may find it more difficult to monitor or manage a number of accounts, particularly at tax time. In this case, investing through a broker or discount brokerage firm may be a better strategy.

Buying Through a Broker or a Financial Planner

The do-it-yourself route isn't for everyone. Many people don't have the time to research funds themselves; others just feel more comfortable following the advice of a financial professional.

SMART SOURCES

Do-It-Yourself Investing

You can invest directly in many of today's best-performing no-load mutual funds. The following fund companies offer toll-free phone access and a wide range of shareholder services:

American Century
800-345-2021

Berger Funds
800-333-1001

Dreyfus
800-645-6561

Fidelity Investments
800-544-8888

Janus
800-525-3713

Neuberger & Berman
800-877-9700

Scudder Funds
800-728-3337

Strong Funds
800-368-1030

T. Rowe Price
800-638-5660

The Vanguard Group
800-662-7447

Putnam: Loaded Opportunities

You'll find Putnam Investments near the top of most mutual fund charts; one of the industry's fastest-growing fund companies, Boston-based Putnam is also home to many of its best-performing investments.

Putnam sells its funds primarily through brokers, and its fees are among the steepest in the industry. But their consistent, team-based approach has obviously struck a chord with investors. Putnam is one of today's mutual fund giants, if not yet in the same league as its crosstown competitor, Fidelity.

Putnam's domestic stock funds are the jewel in its crown; the company also offers highly regarded fixed-income investments as well.

Putnam Investments
888-478-8626
www.putnaminv. com

But advice does come at a price: anywhere from 4 percent to 6 percent of your investment dollars. If you buy through a broker or financial planner, you will typically be offered only load funds (the load pays the broker's commission), unless you hire a fee-based adviser (or invest in a wrap account; see below for more information).

There's certainly nothing wrong with paying a load or paying for financial guidance. Often brokers or planners can offer you a wider array of fund choices (including their own proprietary funds) and more convenience; for example, even if you invest in multiple funds or multiple families, you'll usually receive one consolidated statement—a real benefit at tax time. However, it's important to make sure you're getting what you've paid for: sound advice, solid research, and real service. Don't be afraid to ask for references and actual performance results.

Before You Hire a Financial Adviser:

Remember that a broker or financial planner will always make money—even if you don't. Before you hire a professional to manage your assets, make sure he or she is the right person for you.

1. Does the broker or planner understand your goals? Make sure the investments they recommend match your personal situation and tolerance for risk.

2. How is the planner compensated? Will you have to pay any additional expenses like brokerage costs or account fees?

3. Will you have access to a wide variety of investment products? Planners who offer only one or two fund choices may be working more for the fund company than they are for you.

3. What kind of experience have they had? Ask about their track record in both up and down markets. You should be able to obtain references and copies of reports for similarly situated clients.

4. What are their credentials? Although there are no official educational requirements to become a financial planner, many advisers do have specialized investment training. You may want to look for someone who is qualified as a Certified Financial Planner (CFP) or Chartered Financial Consultant (ChFC). Make sure that whomever you hire has knowledge of taxes, insurance, and estate-and retirement-planning issues.

SMART MONEY

What are the advantages of a mutual fund supermarket? "In one word, flexibility," says Jack White, chairman of the discount brokerage firm that bears his name. White launched the first supermarket-style program in early 1984, realizing that "in practice, no single fund family can offer everything an investor wants; there may be country- or style-specific funds that are only available elsewhere.

Supermarkets provide a conduit to any and all investments. Our philosophy is to provide investors with a full menu so that they can select the funds best suited to their needs."

Many brokers (including firms like Merrill Lynch, Dean Witter, and Paine Webber) are now offering fee-based—rather than commission-oriented—investment guidance. If you prefer to use an independent adviser, referrals to fee-based professionals are available from the National Association of Personal Financial Planners at (800) 366-2732.

What Is a "Wrap" Account?

As consumers have grown more resistant to paying sales commissions, brokers and financial planners have found new ways to make money. Their latest product, the wrap account, assesses a flat percentage of assets, usually 3 percent, rather than charging multiple fees or loads.

For that price, you'll get something resembling your own personal fund of funds: a diversified portfolio of mutual funds, more or less tailored to suit your individual objectives. The broker or planner will act as the overall fund manager, monitoring, rebalancing, and trading in the account in order to meet your goals.

While wrap accounts do offer some advantages, particularly for time-pressed investors, they often require high minimum balances (typically, $50,000 or more). In addition to the broker's flat fee, you may find yourself paying management expenses for each underlying investment—and those can bring your total cost up to as much as 5 percent.

Is the advice worth it? Many investors obviously think so; according to a study by Cerulli Associates and Lipper Analytical Services, mutual fund wrap account assets have now grown to over $19 billion. However, it probably pays to be skeptical: those hefty fees can take a real bite out of your returns. And wrap accounts have been criticized for being much less personalized than they claim. Unless you're gaining access to funds you couldn't buy directly or enjoying consistently outsized performance, you'll probably do better picking funds on your own.

Buying Through a Discount Broker

Discount brokers have been selling mutual funds since the early 1980s, and in that time they have transformed the industry. The "mutual fund supermarkets" pioneered by firms like Charles Schwab and Jack White & Company have attracted millions of new investors and billions of dollars.

The supermarkets offer one-stop shopping, providing easy access to hundreds if not thousands of different funds from multiple fund companies. They allow you to effectively create your own fund family; you can mix loads and no-loads, big names and small upstarts, in a portfolio designed to meet your particular needs. Buying through one channel minimizes paperwork (all your fund investments are consolidated on one statement) and makes it very easy to switch between funds if your objectives change.

You do pay for convenience. Funds purchased through these supermarkets are typically sold with a transaction fee, which can range from $27 at Jack White to $39 at Schwab (these charges can be

SMART SOURCES

You can't beat the fund supermarkets for convenience. Not only can you invest in multiple fund families with only one phone call, you can often do so after market hours and even online. Just make sure that your supermarket carries the fund or fund families you're interested in.

E*Trade
800-786-2573
www.etrade.com

Fidelity Investments
800-544-9697
www.fidelity.com

Charles Schwab
800-435-4000
www.schwab.com/funds

Jack White & Co.
800-233-3411
www.jackwhiteco.com

Waterhouse Securities
800-934-4410
www.waterhouse.com

somewhat reduced, however, if you do your investing online).

In 1992, however, Schwab introduced their Mutual Fund OneSource service, which allows investors to purchase no-load mutual funds without paying any additional commissions. An immediate success with investors, Schwab's program was quickly followed by White's NoFee Network and Fidelity's FundsNetwork; by the end of 1998, other discounters and even banks are expected to get in on the no-fee act.

Despite obvious benefits, the no-fee programs do have their faults. Not every fund or fund family is available; in fact, Vanguard and T. Rowe Price have refused to participate, while Fidelity's funds can be bought without fees only through its own program. And Schwab et al. have been accused of indirectly raising fund expenses: since commissions have been eliminated, the no-fee sponsors are instead compensated by the participating fund company, which may then increase its distribution fees or 12b-1 fees to cover any lost revenue.

Investing through a discounter is meant to make your life easier; before deciding on any firm, you may want to determine just what you'll need. Few discount brokerages offer any individualized guidance (although Fidelity and Schwab do offer planning information via their web sites), and access to investment research can be limited (again, the larger firms provide more services). You may also be charged if you sell funds frequently or hold your securities for only a short time. Be sure you can live with these restrictions, or you may find yourself paying unexpected costs for a "no-fee" investment.

Stagecoach Funds:
Innovative Funds from a Banking Pioneer

You may not know the Stagecoach Funds, but you're sure to have heard of their sponsor. This family of 35 mutual funds is managed by Wells Fargo Bank—the one of Gold Rush fame.

In addition to the standard equity and bond investments, Stagecoach also offers an innovative line of asset allocation funds, the LifePath Portfolios. Each Portfolio has a specific target date. For example, LifePath 2040 is intended for investors who will retire in 2040. The LifePath products are designed to take any guesswork out of investing; unlike other "all-in-one" funds, these automatically readjust their asset mix as time passes, becoming increasingly less aggressive as shareholders close in on their goals. Although the Portfolios have delivered attractive returns so far, critics have complained that LifePath's overall investing strategy—each fund keeps at least a portion of assets in both bonds and cash—is too conservative, particularly for longer term investors.

Stagecoach Fund shareholders who live in the western states served by Wells Fargo banks enjoy an added bonus: You have the option of buying, selling or checking account balances at your convenience, through the bank's extensive ATM network.

Stagecoach Funds
800-222-8222
www.wellsfargo.com

Buying from a Bank

If you already do most of your financial transactions at your local bank, why not invest there, too? That's certainly what the banking industry would like. According to the Investment Company Institute, banks now represent 14 percent of all mutual fund assets—or more than $630 billion.

Investing in small steady amounts may not be an exciting strategy, but for health care investment banker Abigail Franklin, it's an unquestionably successful one. Since 1995, she has invested $100 a month in each of three different mutual funds; today, with relatively little effort, she's amassed a substantial portfolio.

Because Abby follows a dollar cost averaging approach, she's unconcerned about short-term volatility. "If the price drops, it means that I buy more shares," she says.

"Even though I work in the financial arena, I don't trust myself to predict the market's highs or lows," she continues. "And that's the thing about dollar cost averaging—I don't have to think about it.

Banks are certainly the most convenient option for many investors; today, you can even buy or sell shares using your ATM card. However, there are some substantial drawbacks. Banks generally sell load funds; those that offer no-loads typically impose a transaction charge. You'll also find that your choices are rather restricted; while quite a number of banks have launched their own funds, many simply offer a limited selection of the more established families (although NationsBank and Bank of America have recently introduced their own supermarket programs).

If you do decide to buy mutual funds at a bank, it's important to remember that, unlike your checking or savings account, these investments are not protected by any sort of insurance or government guarantee. You're as vulnerable to risk at a bank as you would be with any broker or financial planner or with the fund company itself—but without the range of investment opportunities or price advantages available almost anywhere else.

Shareholder Services: What's Important to You?

To attract shareholders, many fund companies and brokerage firms have begun offering a variety of investing conveniences, usually at no additional cost. While these are definitely secondary considerations, you may want to make sure that you're getting the services you most need before you decide where to invest.

Shareholder services are typically explained in the fund's prospectus or the company's marketing literature; you may also want to ask your representative the following questions.

How Easy Is It to Monitor Your Account?

Make sure you can stay informed about your investment. In addition to quarterly statements and trade confirmations, many firms also provide fund newsletters as well as twenty-four-hour telephone access and trading capabilities. Internet users may also want to check out the company's web site; Fidelity, Vanguard, T. Rowe Price, and Charles Schwab have particularly helpful sites that let you check balances as well as buy and sell fund shares online.

Does the Fund Company or Broker Offer Exchange Privileges?

While it's best to invest for the long term, there are often good reasons to switch from one fund to another. Most companies allow you to move to a different fund within the same family with just a phone call; many will even waive any load charges or redemption fees.

Easy switching is a key advantage of the mutual fund supermarkets as well. In fact, you should have no difficulty exchanging shares even of different fund companies, although you should be advised that some restrictions and transaction fees may apply.

(Exchanging shares of funds often has tax consequences; for more about your potential tax liabilities, see chapter 8.)

Can You Write Checks against Your Account?

Bond and money market funds typically offer check-writing privileges, although there may be a limit to the number of checks you can write; you may also be charged a small fee for the service. In addition to being able to manage your financial transactions with one account, you can usually redeem fund shares simply by writing a check.

What Investment Accounts Are Available?

Many companies, realizing that their investors have multiple goals, now offer a wider array of account options, including custodial, trust, and retirement plans.

Can You Invest Automatically?

Investors who prefer a hands-off approach should ask if the fund company or broker offers an automatic investment program. These allow you to invest a fixed amount of money on a regular basis, typically either monthly or quarterly. The money is automatically deducted from your bank account or payroll check; you don't even have to think about transferring assets.

This type of disciplined investing is also known as *dollar cost averaging*. It's often recommended as a way of smoothing out the effects of market volatility; since you buy more shares when the price is low and fewer when the price rises, you actually make market fluctuations work to your advantage. And you'll end up paying a lower average cost per share.

Can You Choose to Have Your Dividends Automatically Reinvested?

Income funds throw off regular dividend payments. If you don't need this money to pay everyday expenses, you may want to build your investment by using these dividends to buy additional shares of the fund. Many companies offer an automatic reinvestment program; you may have to sign up for it when opening your account. Just remember that even though you aren't receiving the dividends as cash, you do incur tax liabilities. See chapter 8 for more information.

The Best Time to Buy

Don't worry too much about when to buy a fund; the important thing is to get started and put your money to work as soon as you can. While the financial world is notoriously unpredictable, waiting for just the right time to invest is a sure way to miss out on the market's overall gains.

That said, there actually is a best time and even a best day to buy fund shares: the day after a fund distributes capital gains. This typically occurs in late November or December; you can ask your fund representative for a more precise date. You'll find that mutual fund prices tend to rise before the distribution and will *always* fall by a corresponding amount right afterward. More important, these capital gains distributions have significant tax consequences. You may find yourself owing the IRS a hefty amount on an investment you've owned for only a few days (for more about taxes, see chapter 8).

THE BOTTOM LINE

Convenience, advice, selection, and cost: these are the most important factors to consider before you decide where to invest. You'll find that fund companies typically offer the lowest costs, while discount brokerage firms provide the widest array of investment choices.

Competition has made the fund industry more responsive to investors' needs. Shareholder services now include check-writing and exchange privileges, more account options, and easy access to information and balances. An automatic investment plan is an additional convenience—and one that can help you maximize your investing dollars.

CHAPTER 8

Managing Your Invest- ments

THE KEYS

• There are plenty of ways to track your investment. Newspapers, online sites, and automated telephone services give you easy access to fund prices.

• Newspaper quote listings carry a lot of valuable information—if you know how to read them.

• Learn to decode an account statement.

• Picking the right time, and reason, to sell a fund is just as important as selecting the right fund to buy.

• With a few tax-smart strategies, you can minimize your tax exposure.

Investing isn't a onetime event—it's an ongoing process. Once you purchase a fund, you'll want to check periodically to make sure that your investing strategy remains on track.

"Periodically" is the key word here. While it's certainly possible (and for many people, enjoyable) to follow your funds on a daily, weekly, or even monthly basis, most investors are probably better off checking in once a quarter or even once every six months. Too much monitoring can often make you too sensitive to inevitable market fluctuations.

More important than every blip or dip in performance is whether the fund still fits with your overall investment plan. You'll want to make sure that your portfolio still reflects your goals; it may need rebalancing to keep all your investing percentages in the right proportions. Or perhaps your financial circumstances have changed in some way. As we'll see later in this chapter, these are all much better reasons for selling a mutual fund than short-term gains or losses.

Keeping Track of Your Investments

Fortunately, it's easy to monitor your mutual fund investment. Fund prices for hundreds of securities are listed in the financial section of most daily newspapers, and up-to-the-minute information about even more investments can be found on the Internet. Web sites sponsored by Morningstar, Quicken, Charles Schwab, Fidelity, and Yahoo all provide immediate access to fund quotes and

A Regular Checkup

Is your fund keeping up with the competition? It's easy to compare the total returns of similar investments; both Morningstar and the financial magazines frequently publish category averages. However, you may want to be wary if your fund performs *too* well; unusually outsized returns could mean that the fund manager is taking on a lot more risk than his or her peers.

You'll also want to check that your fund's performance is in line with general market trends. There are now a wide array of benchmarks available; make sure you choose the one most appropriate for your particular investment:

Fund Category	Market Index
Large-cap stock funds	S&P 500 Index
Small- and mid-cap funds	Russell 2000 Index
International stock funds	Morgan Stanley Europe, Australia and Far East (EAFE) Index
Emerging market funds	Morgan Stanley Emerging Markets Index
Taxable bond funds	Lehman Brothers Aggregate Bond Index
Tax-exempt bond funds	Lehman Brothers Municipal Bond Index

other data. You can also get daily prices by using the automated phone services offered by many brokerages and mutual fund companies.

Being able to get information on demand has its advantages: you can now research or trade at your own convenience. But while it's tempting to check your funds daily, remember that all investments will fluctuate in value, sometimes quite dramatically. That's why day-to-day changes are rarely indicative of a fund's overall performance.

Instead, many investors prefer to monitor

their funds quarterly, which is when most mutual fund companies will send out account statements. Quarterly data are also the basis for many magazine and newspaper special issues; *Forbes, Fortune, Money, U.S. News & World Report,* and *BusinessWeek* all regularly review mutual fund performance.

Reading Mutual Fund Quotations

Mutual fund prices are quoted in almost all daily newspapers. If your local paper doesn't include fund listings, you can always check nationally distributed publications such as the *Wall Street Journal, USA Today,* or *Investor's Business Daily.*

While there are some variations from paper to paper (and even from day to day), almost all fund quotations will include the fund's net asset value, any sales loads, and the change in share price from the previous day's trading. Additional fees, such as marketing or redemption charges, may also be included; you'll usually find an explanatory note accompanying your newspaper's mutual fund table.

1. You'll find specific funds listed alphabetically, below the fund company name.

2. The NAV tells you how much each share is worth. To calculate the value of your investment, multiply the NAV by the number of shares you own.

3. The offer price is the amount you would pay to purchase shares. It's typically the NAV plus any sales charges.

4. An "NL" in the offer price column means this is a no-load fund.

5. Share prices will fluctuate. The American Express Small Company Growth Fund shown here has gained 42 cents per share since the previous day.

6. A "d" means the American Century New Opportunities Fund charges a redemption fee.

7. Some funds also charge annual 12b-1 fees.

8. Watch for multiple charges. This fund imposes both redemption and 12b-1 fees.

Fund	Sales Load	NAV	1-day Net Chg
AAL A			
Bond m	4.00	9.98	+.03
CapGrow m	4.00	28.12	+.54
EqInc m	4.00	13.71	+.17
HiYld m	4.00	10.32	-.01
Intl m	4.00	10.81	+.05
MidCap m	4.00	15.35	+.19
MuniBond m	4.00	11.46	+.01
SmCapStk m	4.00	13.25	+.19
AARP Investment			
BalStkBd	NL	21.63	+.22
BdfdxInc	NL	15.24	+.03
CapGrow	NL	57.02	+.94
DivrGrow	NL	18.06	+.18
DivrInc p	NL	16.98	+.08
GNMAUSTrs	NL	15.21	+.04
GloGrow	NI	19.23	+.20
GrowInc	NL	57.79	+.83
HQBd	NL	16.16	+.02
InsTaxFBd	NL	18.48	..
IntlStk	NL	18.20	-.17
SmCpStk	NL	20.80	+.20
USStkIdx	NL	19.95	+.37
AIM A			
AggGrow m	5.50	49.40	+.83
Bal m	4.75	27.13	+.28
BlChip m	5.50	34.72	+.67
CapDev m	5.50	15.81	+.23
Charter m	5.50	13.19	+.22
Constell m	5.50	28.40	+.51
GloAgg m	4.75	18.28	+.22
GloGrw m	4.75	18.04	+.24
GloInc m	4.75	10.96	+.01
CtolUtil m	5.50	19.97	+.23
Grow m	5.50	16.99	+.31
HiYld m	4.75	10.23	-.01
Income m	4.75	8.60	+.02
IntGovt m	4.75	9.43	+.03
IntlEq m	5.50	17.98	+.19
LtdMatRet m	1.00	10.07	+.01
MuniBd m	4.75	8.31	+.01
Summit f	8.50	14.83	+.27
Value m	5.50	34.85	+.56
Weingart m	5.50	21.61	+.41
AIM C			
AdvFlex m	1.00	20.79	+.27
AdvIntlVa m	1.00	15.98	+.27
AdvLroCap m	1.00	25.76	+.46
AdvMulti m	1.00	14.70	+.18
AdvReal m	1.00	15.24	+.05
API			
APIGrow m	NL	13.71	-.19
ASMIdx30			
ASMIdx30 d	NL	19.01	+.27
Accessor			
Growth	NL	23.99	+.63
IntFixIn	NL	12.16	-.0?
IntlEq	NL	15.94	+.21
MtgSec	NL	12.64	+.03
Shortint	NL	12.29	+.01
SmMidCap	NL	24.12	+.42
Valueinc	NL	20.66	+.33
Acorn			
Acorn	NL	18.04	+.19
Intl	NL	20.30	+.18
USA	NL	16.08	+.14
AdsnCa p			
AddisnCa b	NL	32.61	+.51
Advance Capital I			
Balanced b	NL	16.35	+.20
EqGrow b	NL	18.73	+.33
RetInc b	NL	10.61	+.04
Advantus			
Bond A m	5.00	10.49	+.03
CornrstA m	5.00	16.50	+.15
EnterprA m	5.00	15.47	+.22
HorizonA m	5.00	23.17	+.54
IntlBal m	5.00	11.78	+.07
MtgSec A m	5.00	10.63	+.02
SpectrmA m	5.00	16.47	+.74
VentureA m	5.00	12.71	+.19
Aetna I			
Aetna	NL	12.75	+.15
Ascent	NL	12.24	+.13
Bond	NL	10.21	+.02
Crossrds	NL	12.01	+.10
Grow	NL	16.09	+.31
GrowInc	NL	16.22	+.26
IntlGrow	NL	11.96	+.14
InvAmer m	5.75	18.47	+.14
IntlBdAm m	4.75	13.47	+.02
InvCoAm m	5.75	29.87	+.09
Mutual m	5.75	30.76	+.39
NewEcon m	5.75	21.94	+.46
NewPersp m	5.75	21.33	+.31
CapWorld m	5.75	27.62	+.27
TaxEBdAm m	4.75	17.43	..
TaxECA m	4.75	16.36	+.01
USGovSec m	4.75	13.17	+.03
WAMutInv m	5.75	32.65	+.52
American Cent-20thC			
Giftrust	NL	24.64	+.64
GrowthInv	NL	26.17	+.57
HeritInv	NL	12.57	+.18
IntlDisc d	NL	9.13	-.06
IntlGrInv	NL	9.05	+.15
NewOpp d	NL	5.58	+.10
SelectInv	NL	46.33	+.95
UltraInv	NL	30.14	+.68
VistaInv	NL	13.05	+.22
American Cent-Benham			
BondInv	NL	9.64	+.02
CAInsTxF	NL	10.38	+.01
CAIntTxF	NL	11.24	+.01
CALgTxF	NL	11.48	+.01
CALtdTxF	NL	10.35	..
CAMuHiYld	NL	9.73	+.01
GNMA Inv	NL	10.68	+.03
IntBd	NL	10.04	+.02
IntTaxF	NL	10.48	+.01
IntTrsIv	NL	10.56	+.03
IntlBd	NL	11.03	-.02
LgTmTrs	NL	10.50	+.07
LgTmTxF	NL	10.71	..
ShTmGovt	NL	9.46	..
ShTmTrsIv	NL	9.80	..
TarMat00	NL	88.79	+.13
TarMat05	NL	67.97	+.31
TarMat10	NL	52.75	+.28
TarMat15	NL	42.22	+.34
TarMat20	NL	30.55	+.30
TarMat25	NL	25.21	+.31
American Century			
Bal	NL	19.02	+.26
EqGrowInv	NL	21.08	+.35
EqIncInv	NL	7.01	+.07
GloGold	NL	6.39	+.07
GlbNatRes	NL	11.69	+.06
IncGrInv	NL	26.65	+.47
RealEstIv	NL	15.67	+.06
StrAlcAgg	NL	6.44	+.08
StrAlcCon	NL	5.49	+.04
StrAlcMod	NL	6.13	+.05
Utilities	NL	14.68	+.22
Val Inv	NL	7.45	+.09
American Expr IDS A			
BlChip f	5.00	10.15	+.19
Bond f	5.00	5.22	+.01
CATaxE f	5.00	5.33	..
Discover f	5.00	12.65	+.17
DivrEqInc f	5.00	9.97	+.17
EmgMkt f	5.00	6.20	-.05
EqSelect f	5.00	14.66	+.25
ExtraInc f	5.00	4.60	..
FedInc f	5.00	5.07	+.02
GloBal f	5.00	5.66	+.06
GloBond f	5.00	6.12	..
GloGrow f	5.00	7.63	+.12
Growth f	5.00	34.20	+.57
HiYldTxE f	5.00	4.66	+.01
InsTaxE f	5.00	5.60	..
Intl f	5.00	11.05	+.09
MgdAlloc f	5.00	11.55	+.14
Mutual f	5.00	14.38	+.19
NewDimen f	5.00	25.64	+.49
ProcMet f	6.00	6.50	+.05
Progress f	5.00	10.07	+.14
ResOpp f	5.00	6.70	+.13
Select f	5.00	9.17	+.03
SmCoIdx f	5.00	7.05	+.10
Stock f	5.00	25.96	+.48
TaxEBd f	5.00	4.13	..
UtilInc f	5.00	8.63	+.11
American Expr IDS B			
EqValue m	5.00	12.41	+.21
StratAgg m	5.00	20.36	+.41
American Expr Strat			
Grow m	NL	36.12	+.60
GrowTren m	NL	28.42	+.54
SmCoGrA m	4.50	21.74	+.42
BJB			
BJBIntlA b	NL	15.43	+.19
BNY Hamilton Inst			
IntGovt N	NL	9.87	+.02
IntlvGrad b	NL	10.43	+.03
IntTxE b	NL	10.21	..
IntlEq b	NL	11.70	+.16
LgCapGr b	NL	11.71	+.16
SmCapGr b	NL	12.36	+.19
BNYEqInlv			
BNYEqInlv b	NL	16.26	+.20
IntGovt b	NL	9.87	+.02
BT Inv			
AstMgt b	NL	14.17	+.20
CapApr	NL	13.07	+.24
EqApr	NL	15.96	+.29
GloHY	NL	10.86	+.02
IntTxF b	NL	10.72	..
IntlEq	NL	22.21	+.38
LatAm	NL	14.21	+.25
LifGr b	NL	14.24	+.20
LifMid b	NL	12.10	+.13
LifSht b	NL	10.54	+.08
LtdTm	NL	9.85	+.01
PacBasEq	NL	5.79	+.01
SmCap	NL	19.55	+.25
Babson			
Bond L	NL	1.56	..
Bond S	NL	9.82	+.01
Enterp	NL	19.28	+.12
EnterpII	NL	25.80	+.18
Growth	NL	19.78	+.39
ShadwStk	NL	13.25	+.09
SthvoIntl	NL	18.97	+.13
TaxFInc	NL	9.17	..
TaxFIncS	NL	10.79	..
Value	NL	50.24	+.74
Baird			
BairdAdj m	3.25	8.76	..
Baron			
Asset b	NL	51.05	+.72
GrowInc b	NL	25.93	+.35
SmCap b	NL	11.22	+.09
Bartlett			
BasicValA m	4.75	20.17	+.32
Euro A m	4.75	24.41	+.30
ValIntlA m	4.75	13.01	+.14
Bear Stearns			
EmgMkt A b	3.75	11.89	+.05
InsiderA m	4.75	17.27	+.22
S&PStarA m	4.75	19.11	+.50
SmCapValA m	4.75	22.21	+.27
Berger			
100 b	NL	15.47	+.16
Bal b	NL	13.00	+.12
GrowInc b	NL	14.31	+.25
NewGen b	NL	14.78	+.33
3xOCoCrow b	NL	4.91	+.11
Bernstein			
CAMuni	NL	13.95	+.01
DivrMuni	NL	13.78	+.01
EmgMkt d	NL	16.41	+.02
GovShDur	NL	12.53	..
IntDur	NL	13.23	+.03
IntlVal	NL	19.70	+.24
ShDurCA	NL	12.56	..
ShDurPlu	NL	12.44	+.01
Berwyn			
Berwyn d	NL	22.74	+.21
Income	NL	12.79	+.06
Bhirud			
ApexMCap m	5.75	7.56	-.01
BlackRock Inv			
Bal A m	4.50	18.43	+.27
Boston 1784			
AstAlluc b	NL	14.93	+.18
Grow b	NL	12.93	+.16
GrowInc b	NL	20.25	+.22
Income b	NL	10.18	+.03
IntlEq b	NL	12.82	+.13
ShTmInc b	NL	10.09	+.01
TaxEMdTm b	NL	10.42	+.01
USGovMed b	NL	9.55	+.02
BostonBal			
BostonBal	NL	27.50	+.46
Bramwell			
BramwelGr b	NL	20.99	+.39

Source: San Francisco Chronicle

Understanding Your Mutual Fund Statement

Account statements can vary tremendously from company to company. Fidelity, Janus, and Vanguard provide remarkably useful documents; in addition to showing your balances and how much your investments have gained or lost since the previous quarter, these statements also include income summaries and a breakdown of taxable and nontaxable accounts. In addition, these companies consolidate all of your fund holdings onto one statement—a real bonus at tax time; other firms may send you a separate statement for each fund you own.

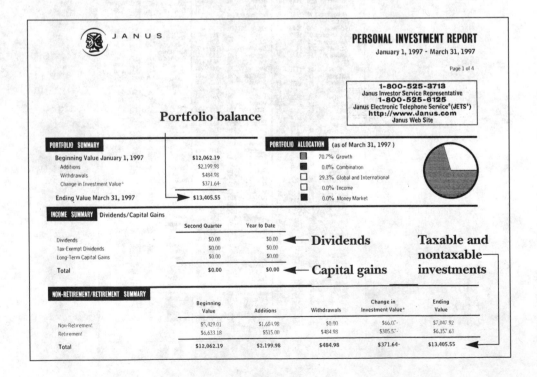

JANUS

PERSONAL INVESTMENT REPORT
January 1, 1997 – March 31, 1997

Page 2 of 4

FUND SUMMARY

Change in value

NON-RETIREMENT	Beginning Value	Additions	Withdrawals	Change in Investment Value*	Ending Value
41-Janus Worldwide Fund	$ 2,673.17	$ 1,084.98	$ 0.00	$ 170.70	$ 3,928.85
42-Janus Fund	$ 1,078.56	$ 300.00	$ 0.00	$ 15.04-	$ 1,363.52
45 Janus Venture Fund	$ 1,677.28	$ 300.00	$ 0.00	$ 221.73-	$ 1,755.55
Subtotal	$ 5,429.01	$ 1,684.98	$ 0.00	$ 66.07-	$ 7,047.92
NON-RETIREMENT TOTAL	$ 5,429.01	$ 1,684.98	$ 0.00	$ 66.07-	$ 7,047.92
RETIREMENT					
43-Janus Twenty Fund	$ 990.43	$ 0.00	$ 0.00	$ 15.87	$ 1,006.30
48-Janus Mercury Fund	$ 5,642.75	$ 515.00	$ 484.98	$ 321.44-	$ 5,351.33
Subtotal	$ 6,633.18	$ 515.00	$ 484.98	$ 305.57-	$ 6,357.63
RETIREMENT TOTAL	$ 6,633.18	$ 515.00	$ 484.98	$ 305.57-	$ 6,357.63
GRAND TOTAL	$ 12,062.19	$ 2,199.98	$ 484.98	$ 371.64	$ 13,405.55

1997 Participant Contributions	$ 515.00	1996 Participant Contributions	$ 2,220.00

JANUS

PERSONAL INVESTMENT REPORT
January 1, 1997 – March 31, 1997

Page 3 of 4

TRANSACTION DETAIL

	Date	Transaction Description	Number of Shares	X	Price/ Share =	Dollar Amount	Share Balance
NON-RETIREMENT							

Cost basis

	Date	Transaction Description	Number of Shares	X	Price/ Share =	Dollar Amount	Share Balance
41-Janus Worldwide Fund	01/01/97	Beginning Balance	79.346		$ 33.69	$ 2,673.17	79.346
	01/20/97	Automatic Purchase -ACH	5.750		$ 34.78	$ 200.00	85.096
	01/28/97	Shs Purchased - Good Funds	6.385		$ 34.77	$ 222.00	91.481
	01/28/97	Shs Purchased - Good Funds	7.563		$ 34.77	$ 262.98	99.044
	02/20/97	Automatic Purchase -ACH	5.583		$ 35.82	$ 200.00	104.627
	03/20/97	Automatic Purchase -ACH	5.734		$ 34.88	$ 200.00	110.361
	03/31/97	Ending Balance	110.361		$ 35.60	$ 3,928.85	110.361
42-Janus Fund	01/01/97	Beginning Balance	44.113		$ 24.45	$ 1,078.56	44.113
	01/20/97	Automatic Purchase -ACH	3.968		$ 25.20	$ 100.00	48.081
	02/20/97	Automatic Purchase -ACH	3.843		$ 26.02	$ 100.00	51.924
	03/20/97	Automatic Purchase -ACH	3.981		$ 25.12	$ 100.00	55.905
	03/31/97	Ending Balance	55.905		$ 24.39	$ 1,363.52	55.905
45-Janus Venture Fund	01/01/97	Beginning Balance	31.611		$ 53.06	$ 1,677.28	31.611
	01/20/97	Automatic Purchase -ACH	1.884		$ 53.09	$ 100.00	33.495
	02/20/97	Automatic Purchase -ACH	2.011		$ 49.72	$ 100.00	35.506
	03/20/97	Automatic Purchase -ACH	2.086		$ 47.93	$ 100.00	37.592
	03/31/97	Ending Balance	37.592		$ 46.70	$ 1,755.55	37.592

JANUS

Nontaxable Income

↓

PERSONAL INVESTMENT REPORT

January 1, 1997 - March 31, 1997

Page 4 of 4

TRANSACTION DETAIL

	Date	Transaction Description	Number of Shares	X	Price/ Share	=	Dollar Amount	Share Balance
RETIREMENT								
43-Janus Twenty Fund	01/01/97	Beginning Balance	36.055		$ 27.47		$ 990.43	36.055
	03/31/97	Ending Balance	36.055		$ 27.91		$ 1,006.30	36.055
48-Janus Mercury Fund	01/01/97	Beginning Balance	341.571		$ 16.52		$ 5,642.75	341.571
	01/06/97	1997 Participnt Cont-ACH	11.025		$ 16.78		$ 185.00	352.596
	01/28/97	Excess Contribution Return	12.914-		$ 17.19		$ 222.00-	339.682
	01/28/97	Contrib Return - Earnings	2.384-		$ 17.19		$ 40.98-	337.298
	01/28/97	Ee Exc OTP	12.914-		$ 17.19		$ 222.00-	324.384
	02/05/97	1997 Participnt Cont-ACH	9.740		$ 16.94		$ 165.00	334.124
	03/05/97	1997 Participnt Cont-ACH	9.792		$ 16.85		$ 165.00	343.916
	03/31/97	Ending Balance	343.916		$ 15.56		$ 5,351.33	343.916

*Change in Investment Value represents the appreciation or depreciation of your investment as well as dividend and capital gain distributions.

This material must be preceded or accompanied by a Janus prospectus. Read it carefully before investing. Past performance is no guarantee of future results. Investment results and principal value will fluctuate so that shares, when redeemed, may be worth more or less than their original cost. Please retain for your records. Janus Distributors, Inc. is a Distributor for the Funds and acts as Agent.

What should you look for on an account statement? Make sure you understand any changes in fund values; these can signal potential problems or a need to rebalance your overall portfolio. You'll also want to keep an eye out for any taxable events, like dividends or capital gains distributions.

When Should You Sell Your Fund?

The most successful investors take a long-term perspective. They know that markets can move both up *and* down, and that the value of their funds can easily fluctuate, particularly in the short term.

There is a difference between a temporary setback and truly poor performance. While most financial experts recommend a buy-and-hold strategy, there are some valid reasons to sell a mutual fund.

Your Investing Goals Have Changed

Every fund you choose should fit into your overall investment plan. Obviously, as your personal situation changes—you get closer to retirement, your children graduate from college, or you simply need the money—your investing goals will, too. Don't hesitate to reevaluate your portfolio; selling funds in order to reinvest in others more appropriate to your current needs simply makes good financial sense.

The Fund Chronically Underperforms Either the Market or Its Peers

Even great funds have been known to stumble occasionally. While it may be difficult to stomach, a bad quarter or even a bad year isn't a reason to unload your fund. However, if the fund consistently lags its competitors for more than a year—two at the most—you should probably sell and reinvest your proceeds elsewhere.

Always try to figure out why your fund is faltering; if the fundamentals are solid but the fund's strategy is simply out of favor with the current market, you should probably just be patient. Remember that styles come and go; you may actually be sitting on a soon-to-be-rediscovered gem.

SMART DEFINITION

Buy and Hold
An investing strategy that emphasizes buying a fund and holding on to it for the long term, rather than jumping in and out of the market as a response to short-term movements.

SMART MONEY

Before making any investing decision, look at the big picture, says Matthew Muehlbauer, research manager for the Value Line Mutual Fund Survey. "Always evaluate why you bought a fund in the first place. If the fund is doing what it's supposed to, and your reasons for investing are still valid, then you should hold on to it.

"There will always be some asset classes that underperform and others that outperform. If your fund is in one of those underperforming classes, that's not necessarily a reason to sell. At some point, it will recover."

The Fund Has Switched Strategies

Did you invest in an income fund only to discover that the manager has developed a fondness for more volatile technology stocks? Don't even hesitate: including this fund in your portfolio will not only throw off your asset allocation plan, but may expose you to unexpected and unnecessary risk.

The Fund Manager Changes

Managerial changes in and of themselves aren't a reason to switch investments (particularly not for team-managed funds). However, they are a sign that you should probably monitor the fund more closely for the next few quarters. Make sure that the new manager adheres to the fund objective; unless performance dramatically suffers, there's typically little reason to move on.

How to Sell Fund Shares

Selling fund shares is easy: the fund itself is required to buy back your shares at the current market value. This, of course, can fluctuate. Depending on when you sell, you may receive less or more than you originally paid.

You can usually redeem fund shares with a telephone call. The fund or broker can either send you the proceeds or deposit the cash directly with your bank. If you're redeeming fixed-income or money market fund shares, you can often write yourself a check against your account. Wire transfers, which are usually recommended for large withdrawals, are also an option.

Before making any redemption, you may want to ask if a signature guarantee is required. If so, a bank officer or brokerage representative would have to authenticate your signature, which can delay your sale.

The Dangers of Market Timing

Market timing is the exact opposite of a buy-and-hold strategy. Instead of investing for the long term, market timers will buy and sell on the basis of daily market movements.

The idea is a simple one: by catching upturns and avoiding the worst declines, market timers hope to enjoy increased returns. In reality, it's nearly impossible to predict the market—even for professional investors. By jumping in and out of investments, you simply run a greater risk of buying at a fund's peak or selling at its lowest point.

Fortunately, many studies have shown that simply staying invested—even through dramatic downturns—results in far better returns than trying to outsmart the market. Numbers generated by Ned Davis Research have shown that investors who were fully invested in stocks from January 1, 1986, through December 31, 1995—a ten-year period that included both the market crash of 1987 and the downturn of 1994—actually enjoyed a 14.8 percent annualized return. Missing just the

SMART DEFINITION

Market Timing
This strategy calls for buying stocks when the market begins rising, and selling when you think it's about to fall. However, markets are notoriously unpredictable; the best trading days often occur right after the worst declines. By trying to avoid a market downturn, you're more likely to miss an upturn as well.

F.Y.I.

Every investment decision has tax consequences. Before you place a trade, you may want to calculate the impact a sale will have on your tax bill.

10 best trading days of that decade would have dropped your returns to 10.2 percent. Missing the 40 best days—40 days out of a total 2,526—would have reduced your gains to just 2.5 percent.

Mutual Funds and Taxes

There are many advantages to investing in mutual funds. However, simplifying your tax bill isn't one of them. Even the most straightforward funds can be a tax headache; tax-exempt and foreign funds arc even more complicated.

Part of the problem is simply the way mutual funds are structured. Funds are required by law to pay out virtually all dividends, interest income, and capital gains earned each year. By passing on these earnings to their shareholders, funds also pass on their tax liability: you, rather than the fund's management, get to pay any taxes that are due (unless you've invested in a money market fund or a tax-deferred account like an IRA).

Not only that, but you're often taxed in two ways: on the earnings the fund makes while you're a shareholder (such as gains realized when the fund sells its holdings at a profit), and on any money you make when you redeem your investment. You can even owe taxes when your fund loses money; as long as the fund paid out taxable capital gains during the year, you're liable come April.

Unfortunately, nothing is simple when it comes to mutual funds and taxes. In fact, the amount you owe can vary tremendously, depending on the type of distribution made and even your choice

Merrill Lynch: A Bull in a Bear Market

The bull is the symbol of Merrill Lynch, and it fits this Wall Street power-house. Not only is Merrill the sixth largest mutual fund company (with more than 130 proprietary funds), it's also a full-service brokerage house, financial adviser, and securities underwriter.

Merrill's funds rarely make any top ten lists; ironically, the company's value-oriented offerings tend to shine brightest not in bull markets, but in bearish ones. Conservative and solid—some might say stolid—the company has delivered consistently positive, if not eye-popping, results. Merrill also prides itself on its risk management strategies; quite a number of its funds, including the flagship Basic Value Fund, are substantially less volatile than the market itself.

Merrill Lynch Funds
800-637-3863
www.plan.ml.com

of accounting method. For example, dividends and short-term capital gains (sales of securities held less than one year) are typically taxed as ordinary income—which means some investors could pay as much as 39.6 percent on any proceeds. And thanks to recent tax changes, long-term capital gains can be taxed at a rate of either 20 percent (for securities owned more than eighteen months) or 28 percent (for securities held more than one year but less than eighteen months).

Fund companies are required to send shareholders information about their distributions; these year-end statements should indicate which of your shares are taxed at which rate.

Calculating Gains and Losses

A capital gain (or loss, for that matter) is simply the difference between how much you paid for a security and how much you sold it for. But things are never quite that straightforward when it comes to the IRS. They've devised four different ways to figure out investment gains or losses; since each method can result in surprisingly dissimilar results, you'll want to pick the approach most favorable to your own situation.

First In, First Out (FIFO)

Unless you specify otherwise, the IRS will assume that the first shares you're selling were the first ones you purchased. Because these shares have had the most time to appreciate, this approach typically results in the highest gain and the heaviest tax burden.

Specific Shares

This method lets you declare exactly which shares are sold. However, you'll need to identify—in writing and in advance—the specific shares you're selling. Just send your fund company a written request indicating the number of shares to redeem, the date they were purchased, and the cost basis or purchase price.

Although the specific-shares method requires

more documentation, it allows you the most control over your tax situation. Make sure, though, that you've kept records of all your purchases, including reinvestments, showing both the date and your purchase price. Your fund company may be able to help you re-create some of this documentation.

Average Cost/Single Category

This is one of the easiest methods available to investors. You simply divide the total paid for all your shares by the number of shares owned to arrive at an average cost per share. The single-category method considers all your shares as one purchase, no matter how long you've owned them.

Average Cost/ Double Category

Rather than calculating a single average cost, you come up with two: one for short-term shares and a second for long-term holdings. You can then decide which group you want to sell; like the specific-shares approach, identifying particular securities can give you more control over your final tax bill.

Whichever average cost method you choose, though, must be used for all future sales or exchanges of that security. However, if you own more than one fund, you're allowed to use a different approach for each.

SMART DEFINITION

Cost Basis
The cost basis is simply the purchase price of a security, including any commissions or load charges. Cost basis is then subtracted from the sales price to determine any capital gain or loss.

Tax Reporting

Whenever you sell shares in a mutual fund (even if you simply switch funds), you're creating a "taxable event." Any gains or losses you realize must be reported to the IRS.

While it is your responsibility to keep records of all your mutual fund transactions (even shares purchased by reinvesting dividends), your fund company or broker should be able to provide you with most of the information you need to calculate your tax obligations. In addition to purchase confirmations and quarterly statements, fund companies also send out year-end tax documents known as Form 1099-DIV. These will show your dividend income and capital gains distributions for the year. If you sold fund shares at any time, you'll also receive a Form 1099-B. Typically, these documents are mailed at the end of January for the previous tax year.

Minimizing Taxes

Taxes should be at least a minor consideration when you choose an investment; high tax bills can take a surprisingly big chunk out of a fund's actual annual returns.

Fortunately, there are relatively easy ways to minimize your tax burden; investing in a tax-deferred account, investing in index funds or tax-exempt funds, and just holding on to your investments have all been shown to decrease your tax exposure.

Tax Tip #1: Make Tax-Deferred Investments

The easiest way to minimize your current taxes is to invest through a qualified tax-deferred account like an Individual Retirement Account (IRA) or your company's 401(k) plan.

No taxes are due on any earnings in these accounts until you withdraw your money. At that time, you'll owe ordinary income taxes, but your money will have had years to grow without any penalty. Roth IRAs, introduced in tax year 1998, are another alternative. While they won't lessen your present tax bill (you have to pay taxes on your annual contributions), you'll enjoy both tax-free growth and, ultimately, completely tax-free withdrawals.

The Taxman Cometh

While you should always consult a tax adviser about your individual situation, there are some tax-filing instructions that apply to all mutual fund investors. Here are some examples: You'll need to record ordinary dividends on IRS Form 1040, line 9. If the total of your dividend distributions exceeds $400, you must also complete Schedule B. Long-term capital gain distributions are reported on IRS Form 1040, line 13. You may also need to complete Schedule D.

In addition to the publications available through the IRS, Vanguard puts out a helpful brochure titled "Reporting of Mutual Fund Distributions." For a free copy, call 800-662-7447, or visit their web site www.vanguard.com.

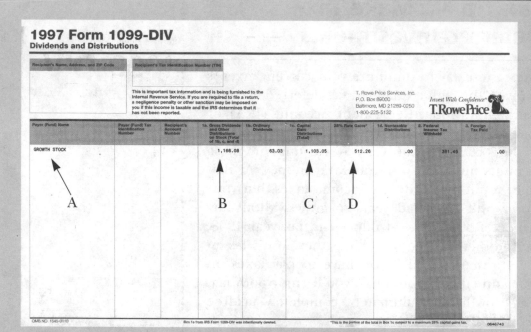

Source: T. Rowe Price Associates, Inc.

A) You'll need to list all your mutual fund investments separately on your tax forms.

B) If you've earned more than $400 in dividends and distributions, you must report the total amount on line 5 of Schedule B (Form 1040).

C) All capital gains distributions must be reported on Schedule D.

D) Long-term capital gains are taxed at a lower rate.

Tax Tip #2: Time Your Purchases

Try not to invest in a mutual fund until *after* it makes a distribution. Otherwise you have to pay taxes on the fund's yearly gains, even if you've owned shares in it only for a short time.

Most fund companies can tell you at least the approximate timing and amount of coming distributions so you can plan your investments. Typically, fund distributions occur in November or December.

Tax Tip #3: Invest for the Long Haul

Just holding on to your investments for more than eighteen months can nearly halve your tax bill. Long-term capital gains are taxed at a rate of just 20 percent—quite an improvement over a short-term tax rate of as much as 39.6 percent.

Tax Tip #4: Invest in Index Funds or Funds with Low Portfolio Turnover

A buy-and-hold strategy is just as important for a mutual fund as it is for an individual investor. Funds that trade frequently will often generate more capital gains—and, consequently, higher taxes.

Not surprisingly, passively managed index

THE BOTTOM LINE

Investing doesn't end once you purchase a fund; in fact, that it's just beginning. You'll want to make sure that the fund you've chosen meets your expectations and continues to fit your investment plan.

Successful investors take a long-term approach; however, even they know there are good reasons for selling a fund. Fund manager changes, consistently poor performance, and a switch in investing strategy should make you cautious. But every sale has tax consequences. To minimize your tax exposure, you may want to invest in a tax-deferred account, or buy index funds or even tax-exempt securities.

Ultimately, though, the smartest thing you can do is simply get started. Because one thing *is* guaranteed in the financial world: The sooner you begin investing, the sooner you'll reach your goals.

funds are among the most tax-efficient. With average turnover rates at somewhere below 20 percent (as compared to the typical equity fund's 82 percent), index funds will often have almost nonexistent tax bills.

Another tax-friendly alternative to consider is a tax-managed mutual fund. This is a relatively new category; there are perhaps a dozen or so now available. Tax-managed funds employ a number of strategies to minimize their (and your) tax exposure, including reducing turnover, buying low-yielding securities, and offsetting any capital gains with well-timed capital losses.

But don't think you should avoid actively managed funds or those with high turnover—funds that deliver high pretax returns usually deliver high after-tax results as well. If you are interested in a fund with aggressive trading strategies but are concerned about the tax consequences, you may want to purchase it through your IRA or another type of tax-advantaged account.

Tax Tip #5: Invest for Tax-Exempt Income

The interest generated by municipal bond funds is free from federal and, in some cases, state and local taxes. But be careful: while the income you earn may be tax-exempt, you'll still owe taxes on any realized capital gains.

Muni funds aren't for everyone. Since they pay lower yields as a trade-off for their tax advantages, unless you're in a particularly high bracket (more than 28 percent), you'll probably realize greater overall gains by investing in taxable funds.

Index

Books in the
Smart Guide™ Series

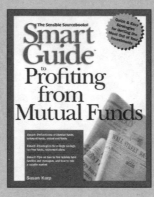

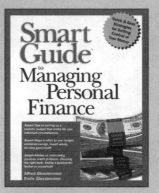

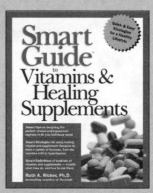